THE AMAZON JUNGLE

ENDORSEMENTS FOR *THE AMAZON JUNGLE*

"Everyday thousands of new sellers join the Amazon marketplace because a friend of theirs said they should. Most of them fail. Jason and Rick have written this book so you could triumph; because when it comes to selling on Amazon, they've done it, they've seen it, and now, they've explained it. Read this book."

Juozas Kaziukenas, Founder, Marketplace Pulse

"The combination of Jason's Amazon street smarts with Rick's lifetime of success in direct marketing makes this a must-read for anyone looking to launch a new brand or products on Amazon."

Bernie Thompson, Founder of Plugable Technologies, the leading brand on Amazon for USB laptop docks

"Selling on Amazon is hard. But it's a whole lot easier once you follow the step-by-step guide in *The Amazon Jungle*. This book has everything you need to know, from the basics to the seriously clever for which you'd usually pay thousands to learn about. Whether Amazon is your side-hustle, your everything, or it sits alongside your own eCommerce store—you need this book!"

Chloe Thomas, Best Selling Author, *eCommerce Marketing,* and host of the award-winning eCommerce MasterPlan and Keep Optimising Podcasts

"Jason's extensive background as both an Amazon seller and consultant provides him with the right perspective to advise brands who sell on Amazon. His keen insights into the potential obstacles that companies face, either in their dealings with competitors or when communicating with performance and policy teams, help new marketplace businesses thrive. In a business climate where mistakes are hugely detrimental to a brand's success, Jason understands the perils of an account suspension and how to prepare for one. We refer clients to Jason because he knows the gratification and the struggles of selling on a competitive platform like Amazon."

Chris McCabe, Founder, eCommerceChris.com
and former Amazon employee on the Performance
and Policy Enforcements Team

"Finally, a book that describes the inside knowledge of how to work the Amazon platform. If your business uses Amazon as a channel, then you need to read this book. It's the map that will bring you to your objectives."

Jim Schleckser, Best Selling Author, *Great CEOs are Lazy,*
and CEO of the Inc CEO Project

"As a long-time successful Amazon Seller, it has become increasingly clear selling and making money on Amazon is becoming harder as the rate of change and challenges on Amazon is increasing at an exponential rate. Jason's in the trenches, hands-on experience building a larger Amazon seller business and consulting with numerous other Sellers, has made Jason one of the most knowledgeable people in the Amazon seller space. Anyone who is currently selling on Amazon or contemplating selling on Amazon, needs a guide like this book to help you navigate *The Amazon Jungle.* Jason and this book are your Jungle Guide."

Jerry Kavesh CEO, 3P Marketplace Solutions

"The book Jason and Rick wrote is a must read. With Amazon.com gobbling up market share and sales, it's a jungle that we must learn how to navigate in the future. Being a 3rd Party seller myself and reading his book. I wish I would have read when I started selling on Amazon. It could have saved me hundreds of thousands of dollars, significant time and stress."

Avais Ahmed, Founder & CEO, Shoeta, Amazon Marketplace Seller
With over 1 Million pairs of shoes sold on Amazon

"A refreshingly knowledgeable read. Jason and Rick have put together a definitive guide to what every start-up and established brand should know to succeed on Amazon. A clear and actionable insight into the complexities of the marketplace and how it should fit with your strategy."

Stuart Conroy, Owner ACTIVE8, Online Growth Agency

"I've been selling on Amazon for four years and staying fresh on the latest strategies has been key to my success. Jason and Rick both really know their stuff here and I never pass up an opportunity to consume the information they put out about Amazon marketing."

Danny Carlson, CEO, Kenji ROI/Actualize Freedom Podcast

"I've known and worked with both Jason and Rick for several years. Their understanding of Amazon and product marketing is unsurpassed. In *The Amazon Jungle*, they share the secrets that have made both them and their clients successful. As a best-selling author who works with authors, I really appreciate a good book. *The Amazon Jungle* by Jason and Rick falls into that category, I highly recommend it."

Susan Gilbert, Author/Coach/Consultant | Destined for More — creating global platforms for leaders via digital marketing, books, and online visibility.

"Do not venture into the Amazon without a guide—without this survival guide. Whether this is your first expedition or you are seasoned seller, you need this book. Veteran brand building and e-commerce mavens Rick Cesari and Jason Boyce leave no stone unturned in showing you the way to confidently enter the world of Amazon.com. and live to tell about it!"

Rich Goldstein, founder of Goldstein Patent Law, Author of the ABA Consumer Guide to Obtaining a Patent

"This book is your lantern in the dark, a compass that can guide you on the treacherous path through Amazon's e-commerce jungle. A must read for any seller seeking to leverage the indispensable platform that Amazon has become."

Ritu Java, CEO and Co-Founder-PPC Nina

"If you want to win on Amazon you need to read Rick and Jason's latest book, *The Amazon Jungle.* Cesari has a track record of turning DTC products into billion-dollar brands and with Amazon veteran, Jason Boyce, has his finger firmly on the pulse of Amazon's always shifting algorithms. Throw out the old notions of how to run your business and build a brand if you want to compete on Amazon and let this book be your navigator and guide. Just because you sell on Amazon doesn't mean you will make sales or sell significantly more than you are now. *The Amazon Jungle* is an easy, comprehensive, digestible read that will open your eyes and impact your bottom line."

Nancy Trent, Trent & Company, Inc. Marketing Communications

"Rick and Jason are both masters of marketing and marketplaces. They have both successfully launched and helped consult on brands that have built astronomical value. This book is an accelerated guide on how to use their decades of experience while you thrive and avoid pitfalls on your way to making your first million dollars on Amazon."

Neal Mody, Managing Director, Zoic Capital

"The days of surfing Alibaba, shipping products to an Amazon Warehouse, then sitting back while the sales roll in are long gone. But the opportunity to partner with the world's largest marketplace to grow a wildly successful ecommerce business is bigger than ever, if you know the latest expert secrets. This is the book that will put you in the know. Rick is an undisputed master of direct selling, and Jason is one of the most experienced and successful Amazon sellers in the world. *The Amazon Jungle* unselfishly reveals the secrets they're using right now to create success on Amazon.com."

Tommy Schaff, Major League Sales

"I wish I had this book when I was selling my own products on Amazon, it would have saved me a lot of time, headaches and money. If you're selling online and ignoring Amazon as a channel, you do so at your peril. But it can be even more perilous selling on Amazon without knowing what to do. Knowing how to make a killing without getting crushed is the key. Rick and Jason's book should be required reading for both new and experienced e-commerce entrepreneurs and used like a playbook for success. It's easy to understand, extremely effective and highly actionable."

Brad Costanzo, Costanzo Marketing Group

"In *The Amazon Jungle*, Rick Cesari and Jason Boyce skillfully show us how to avoid the frustration and pain when selling our products on Amazon. If your business depends on online sales, *The Amazon Jungle* is a must read, full of expert advice and telling case studies. Don't try and figure it out the hard way. Take advantage of Rick and Jason's years of experience and get your copy today."

Jim Grant, Co-Creator of the Six Minute Webinar, and Co-Founder of Speakers Pathway Coalition, Host of "Your Future Is Now" Radio Show

"Having interviewed both Rick and Jason for a podcast series, I was immediately drawn to how uniquely they approach the world of online marketing and business, applied to Amazon. So much so, that I asked them to create online education for our community, here at WealthFit. If you have the opportunity to spend time with them I strongly encourage it. But if that's not possible, then the next best thing is getting this book and getting inside their heads for how to best navigate the jungle that is Amazon!"

Dustin Mathews, Chief Education Officer, WealthFit

"As Amazon has become increasingly unruly and infested with predators, *The Amazon Jungle* is a guide to not just surviving but thriving. Whether you are selling your first product or the 1000th, or thinking about running your first ad or trying to dominate a category, there are sure to be many gems offered by these eminently qualified and battle-scarred authors."

Mina Yoo, CEO, Heroclip; Author, *Be an InventHer: An Everywoman's Guide to Creating the Next Big Thing*

"I knew Rick by reputation even before I met him, and I was already impressed. I had the opportunity to meet him when he spoke at one of our events and my level of respect increased tenfold. Then I read his previous book and knew I would be reading everything he wrote in the future if I wanted to stay current and relevant in the eCommerce space. And now, after having reading his new book, I know that I can recommend it without hesitation. *The Amazon Jungle* is where you turn when you need some reliable, trustworthy guidance and need to build your knowledge base. Rick and Jason know their stuff and enjoy helping entrepreneurs learn from their own past experience. Great read from an interesting and knowledgeable source!"

Melissa Simonson, Empowery eCommerce Cooperative

"Business is no joke, navigating *The Amazon Jungle* alone is ill-advised, and will lead to your own business peril. Having had Rick on my show I can tell you that you're in for a real treat with his attitude, heart, and expertise. Anyone can sell on Amazon, but not everyone can (or does) successfully. It would be wise to start and learn from the best. Putting this wisdom into a book with Jason is a Godsend. Grab a pen, take notes, and enjoy your read."

Mario Fachini, 2x International Best Selling Author, CEO of IWDNow Marketing & Publishing, Host of Expert Authority Effect™ Interviews

"Rick and Jason have forgotten more than most "experts" know about product promotion. *The Amazon Jungle* is the first place I go (and come back to) for success on the largest marketplace in the world."

Ian Garlic, CEO, Authentic Web, Garlic Marketing Show Podcast

"Amazon's spectacular growth and continuous innovation has transformed the retail space all over the world, making disruption the new normal in e-commerce not only in the US, but also in Latin America. Under such a fast changing environment, it became challenging for traditional vendors to generate scalable business ideas. But now, thanks to Jason Boyce and Rick Cesari, third party vendors have a clear guide on how to become successful entrepreneurs in Amazon's vast marketplace. Jason and Rick have untangled the complexities of integrating a successful business model into this vast logistics and product value chain. Through this insightful book, any small vendor can be an Amazon entrepreneur, building successful and profitable brands in this sophisticated globally integrated marketplace."

David Ricardo Suarez, Head of Operations & Shared Services, Grupo Salinas Latam, ESG Investments Advocate|Finance & Business Agility Expert|Leader of High Performance Teams in Latam

"Anyone can list a product on Amazon, but selling successfully requires specific knowledge. Rick Cesari and Jason Boyce lay the road map you need to master the platform."

Liran Hirschkorn, CEO Incrementum Digital

"Selling on Amazon can be successful only if it is not confusing. My transition from retail and infomercials to direct marketing, including Amazon, was initially confusing. However, when I turned to co-author Rick Cesari for help, he made everything clear and simple again. Rick produced our first infomercial for OxiClean Detergent which enabled us to sell our company for $325 million dollars. Even today he continues to help sell our new detergent Powerizer through many channels, including Amazon. Having worked with Rick, I can heartily recommend this book to you."

Max Apppel, Founder of Orange Glo,
OxiClean, and Powerizer detergents

"I have literally read and listened to 100's of business and training books in my career, many boast covering specific topics and others brag to be an overall training to get you going quickly. These publications seldom drill down enough to be helpful once you get going and need answers and an actual strategy. If you are looking to jump into the world of selling on Amazon and looking for a secret weapon to get you up to speed while digging deep enough to answer issues as they arise I am here to tell you that *The Amazon Jungle* is the answer you are looking for, use this book as your Jungle guide and you'll be glad you did!"

Carmine Denisco, Entrepreneur, Inventor, and Author,
The Inventor's Roadmap to Success

THE
AMAZON
JUNGLE

THE TRUTH ABOUT AMAZON

The Seller's Survival Guide for
Thriving on the World's Most Perilous
E-Commerce Marketplace

JASON R. BOYCE
RICK CESARI

NEW YORK

LONDON • NASHVILLE • MELBOURNE • VANCOUVER

The Amazon Jungle

The Truth About Amazon, The Seller's Survival Guide for Thriving on the World's Most Perilous E-Commerce Marketplace

© 2021 Jason R. Boyce & Rick Cesari

Published in New York, New York, by Morgan James Publishing. Morgan James is a trademark of Morgan James, LLC. www.MorganJamesPublishing.com

ISBN 9781631952807 paperback
ISBN 9781631952814 eBook
Library of Congress Control Number: 2020942644

Cover Design by:
Chris Treccani
www.3dogcreative.net

Interior Design by:
Christopher Kirk
www.GFSstudio.com

Morgan James is a proud partner of Habitat for Humanity Peninsula and Greater Williamsburg. Partners in building since 2006.

Get involved today! Visit
MorganJamesPublishing.com/giving-back

To my brothers Ari, Elan, and Josh,
thank you for taking this Amazon journey with me.

TABLE OF CONTENTS

ACKNOWLEDGMENTS

Jason. Although my name is on the cover, the names of my teachers and mentors should be here as well. I couldn't have written this book without their support and encouragement along the way, and it is with the deepest gratitude that I share their wisdom and influence here in these pages. Sometimes starting off is the hardest thing to do and I have Rick Cesari, my co-author, to thank for pushing me to put my thoughts down on paper. Without his kind wisdom, support, and seasoned marketing knowledge, I'm not sure I would have had the confidence to write a book that I believed could make a difference.

No one has guided me more on my Amazon journey than James Thomson, the "Godfather of Amazon Sellers"—a true warrior and champion of small business sellers. James has been there for me time and time again, and he does the same for thousands of other Sellers every day. Sellers, I salute you. I hold you in the highest regard. Your stories inspire me to continue my quest for fairer treatment by Amazon. Throughout this book I use the formal form when referring to Third-Party Sellers out of respect for the hard work and sheer grit that is required of them to survive—even thrive—on the Amazon.com platform.

Family is everything and I have been blessed with two great families. My Mom and Dad gave me life, raised me, and have stood by me through the roughest of times, even when I gave them every reason not to. For that I am forever grateful and especially happy for this opportunity to note it for the public record. And to the Klaristenfelds, my Jewish family from Los Angeles, who taught me a new way. You all gave me the unconditional love and support I needed to see my own potential and pursue my dreams. JB, thank you for standing by my side as we slayed one demon after the next. Last but never least, my most devoted gratitude to my incredible wife, Ann, without whom none of this would be possible. And to our amazing daughters, Maddy and Ellie, who keep me honest, happy, and full of pride every single day. I love you all.

Rick. First and foremost I want to thank Jason Boyce for the time we have spent together exploring one marketing idea after another. He has opened my eyes to this vast new world of Amazon marketing, and we've become good friends in the process. Along the way, I've learned more about the plight of 3P Sellers and how my years of experience in building winning brands is a natural fit for guiding Sellers to profitability on (and off) the Amazon platform. Thanks, too, to Ann Zinn Nikolai, who was part of my team in the early days at Trillium Health Products, and who has dedicated countless hours to helping Jason and I organize and edit this book. Adding Ann to the Friday morning coffee calls was something I looked forward to. Finally, my lovely wife Martha, who is always there to support me and give me space during the early morning hours when my thoughts and ideas flow easily.

Jason and Rick. To Morgan James Publishing, thank you for guiding us through the final steps of this book and for bringing it to market.

FOREWORD

Since Amazon launched its e-commerce marketplace 20 years ago, it has welcomed more than five million third-party sellers to its store, creating one of the largest consumer shopping destinations in the world. In the first few years of this marketplace concept, Amazon repeatedly refined its sales pitch to convince retailers and brands to add massive product selection to its nascent marketplace. By adding enough sellers that more than one would offer the same selection, Amazon kept on recruiting to increase the likelihood of price competition, and hence lower prices that would bring Amazon customers back to open their wallets over and over. Soon, Amazon added its Fulfillment by Amazon program, enabling many sellers with little to no logistics capabilities to turn over the responsibilities of inventory storage and order fulfillment to Amazon, all the while growing their individual seller businesses to become lean operators of multi-million-dollar-a-year businesses.

Such growth brings constant change: in the two decades that have followed, the dynamics on the marketplace have changed significantly. While there are still opportunities to land-grab sales revenue, most of the largest marketplace sellers achieve success by selling their own brands, or exclusively selling other companies' brands. The importance of the brand name is less critical than the seller's intimate knowledge of how the "Amazon sandbox" works, and what Amazon expects from each and every seller on the marketplace. Today, Amazon third-party sellers balance the opportunity to share in billions of dollars of annual sales, with the vicious levels of competition across millions of sellers (not all of whom are playing fairly or legally), compounded by opaqueness and contradiction of Amazon's rather limited communication shared with sellers.

By the time I met Jason Boyce and his brothers in 2007, they were already selling millions of dollars from their own brands, constantly refining and making better than any existing national and international brands—a concept rarely seen back then on Amazon, but now used by tens of thousands of sellers that develop their own "born on Amazon" private-label brands to grab market share from better known brands. I thought Jason and his brothers were a little crazy to be going this route, but every pioneer must suffer through the ignorance of naïve onlookers. I am grateful that I learned from Jason early in my Amazon tenure so I could proselytize the beauty of private-label brands.

A few years later, Rick Cesari spoke at our Prosper Show to a room packed with Amazon private-label sellers, discussing his journey in launching several billion-dollar brands, leveraging television as his primary sales channel. For those in attendance, it was abundantly clear that the secret sauce for uncovering customers' uncommunicated needs, and building brands to meet those needs had been perfected long before the birth of e-commerce by the man onstage!

The adventurous outdoorsman seeking to travel by boat down the 4,000-mile Amazon River will need to understand the full journey, knowledgeable of where the piranhas and bugs will disrupt it. If properly prepared to make the trip, and accepting of the full scope of constant challenges and disruptions, that trip down the river will be rewarding and well worth the time. Becoming a profitable, long-term seller on the Amazon marketplace offers similar personal and financial opportunity. But you will need a toolkit filled with vaccinations, plenty of bug spray, a map, a compass and the right food and water in order to be successful. For sellers of all levels of marketplace experience—*The Amazon Jungle* is that toolkit. I am delighted to recommend the book by Jason and Rick. Read it, dog-ear it, and stay the course.

James Thomson
Mercer Island, Washington

WHY I WROTE THIS

Every day thousands of Amazon Sellers have their small businesses disrupted because their accounts have been accidentally suspended or their listings erroneously removed. I hear about it every time I talk to an Amazon Seller, whether starting up on the platform or doing $30 million a year in sales. In the Amazon e-jungle, the hoops required to jump through to get a problem not-of-your-making resolved are tedious at best, with revenue losses escalating until a solution is reached—sometimes too late. Trust me. The fear is real.

I started selling on Amazon in the pioneering days of e-commerce, when it was a wide-open frontier and an Amazon representative was just a polite phone call away, eager to problem-solve and open to Seller feedback. My brothers and I originally sold other people's products on the platform until Amazon started high-jacking our listings and offering the same products for less. We always expected some push-back from the company, and we were prepared to adapt, switching to products with unique UPC codes. But Amazon always counterpunched by purchasing these exclusives out from under us, after we'd gotten them favorably ranked for search results (of course). We recovered again, building our own private label business, where we dominated the coveted Buy Box, only to have Amazon use our data against us to replicate our best-selling items, then offering their knock-offs at prices as low as our cost.

At every turn, U.S. Third-Party (3P) Sellers are being run-through by Amazon, with the latest example of this found in their relentless pursuit of Chinese national factories. Under their "customer-obsessed" banner to drive down prices, Amazon is recruiting and abetting the same factories 3P Sellers have relied upon, while also stripping away the protective layer provided by these very same Sellers for things like quality-control and consumer product safety.

In Mr. Bezos' preternatural drive to be everything to everyone, he is sacrificing more than just U.S. Third-Party Sellers and the local jobs they create. Amazon shortcuts to price-savings for consumers is removing the critical layers of protection between unsafe, counterfeit products and Amazon shoppers, without culpability. It's the very same argument we hear from Facebook when they claim they are simply a platform with no responsibility to ensure that advertisements or news reports are fact-based. The broken line between Amazon and its Sellers seems to absolve Goliath, while making it nearly impossible for Sellers (and consumers) to seek recourse.

In a recent interview for national television, I was asked about the predicament of Third-Party Sellers. Specifically, the host wanted to know what I would say to Jeff Bezos if he were in the room. It was a tantalizing question for sure; something I hadn't previously considered. In the context of the small recording studio, with bright lights amplifying the prickly question, it felt a lot more real—as if Mr. Bezos was in the room, ready for a debate.

As the second-largest employer in America, millions of people—on and off the Amazon.com platform—have benefited tremendously from what Jeff Bezos has built over the years. Mr. Bezos and his whip-smart teams have fostered the kind of creativity and innovation that offers consumers an extensive selection of choices at unbeatable prices delivered to your door in two days or less. Sellers, like me, have also thrived, despite the hardships, sharpening our entrepreneurial skills and applying our own version of "customer-obsessed."

Pleasantries aside, however, it is 3P Sellers who helped build the Amazon of today and upon whom Mr. Bezos and his company are bound in the future. Bezos alone did not build Amazon; rather, the massive selection and creativity of products and brands are the result of the millions of small entrepreneurs who launched their wares for sale on Amazon. com. I would tell Jeff Bezos that it is unfair and irresponsible to ignore the needs of 3P Sellers by repeatedly thrusting policy changes on them that can put them out of business overnight. I would argue that treating Third-Party Sellers like third-class citizens is not only unconscionable, it's counterproductive to Amazon's own customer-first ambitions because small business owners, and their customers, get screwed in the process. In fact, Amazon 3P Sellers are the largest group of customers of Amazon Services and should share in the benefits of that customer-first culture. Amazon Third-Party Sellers generate 58% of Amazon retail revenue,[1] and according to some analysts such as Scot Wingo, co-founder of ChannelAdvisor, Third-Party Sellers contribute more profits to Amazon's bottom line than the Amazon AWS cloud computing division.[2] And with Mr. Bezos's obsession for the end-customer, they are trampling the folks that

---

1   Felix Richter. "Third-party sellers are outselling Amazon on Amazon," *Statista*. July 22, 2019, https://www.statista.com/chart/18751/physical-gross-merchandise-sales-on-amazon-by-type-of-seller/#:~:text=In%20a%20bid%20to%20 paint,just%203%20percent%20in%201999.

2   Scot Wingo, hosts "Amazon Q4 2019 Earnings Deep Dive." Jason & Scot Show (podcast), January 31, 2020, https://retailgeek.com/jason-scot-show-episode-206-amazon-earnings-q4-2020-deep-dive/.

helped build the business and for which he is still dependent upon for future growth.

Yet in the time it took me to say that, thousands of Third-Party Seller accounts will have been suspended, sometimes indefinitely, due to no fault of their own. Thousands will have had their listings suppressed because Amazon found listings for less on other sales channels. And thousands of U.S. Sellers' high-quality, good-selling product listings will be overrun by a flood of illegitimate and otherwise unsafe products from Chinese factories. How is this okay? I would then beseech Mr. Bezos to meet with a small group of Top Sellers, as any CEO would be convinced to do when a majority faction of their business or a top group of customers is disgruntled. I would urge him to talk with Top Sellers about what is really going on because the total disregard of a company's most productive group of Sellers is unimaginable in the first place. But the ill-treatment, including the deliberate shutdown of Seller accounts and profitable product listings, would not likely be tolerated anywhere else.

The intensity with which I delivered my outburst surprised the host and his crew, and it has since led to deeper conversations about the controversy on a national level. I got my first taste of playing the advocate role for Sellers when my good friend James Thomson, the Godfather of all Amazon Sellers, invited me to speak at the very first Prosper Show. James' first-hand experience as the former business head of Amazon Services and first FBA account manager, primed him to create the Prosper Show, an annual conference bringing thousands of discerning and established Amazon Sellers together once a year to share best practices.

It was at this conference in 2016 that my career path took an unexpected turn. James invited me to join a group of panelists for a session on Amazon selling. But it was what happened after the presentation that was so pivotal. A large group of Sellers who'd attended the talk followed me and a few of the other panelists out of the room and into the hallway. It was like a spontaneous support group, swapping war stories, sharing solutions, trading business cards. This was exactly what James envisioned—where the conference and the networking that followed could be a useful resource for Sellers who face crippling obstacles in their tireless struggle to make a profit on Amazon. Mission accomplished, James.

Since then, I've shifted my focus from seller to advisor. The switch has been profoundly gratifying, using my years of experience on Amazon to help Sellers avoid the same traps that snared my brothers and me; then helping them build winning brands, in spite of Amazon's aggressions. Third-Party Sellers dominate the Amazon retail market, with nearly $43 billion in 3P Seller service revenue, up from $32 billion in the previous year.[3] Even Mr. Bezos noted the trend in his 2019 letter to shareholders, where he acknowledges that Amazon is a smaller player in global retail. "To put it bluntly," he wrote, "Third-party sellers are kicking our first-party butt. Badly."

As a Marine Officer, I learned how to shape my ambition for constant improvement, and I developed the mental toughness and life skills required to bend and adapt under the most difficult of circumstances. I don't expect Amazon to offer 3P Sellers a free lunch, but selling on their platform, while also contributing generously to the company's bottom line, shouldn't be analogous to war.

I wrote this book as a strategic guide for 3P Sellers who want to survive *and thrive*—on Amazon. The steps laid out in these pages are inspired by the *7 Steps to Amazon Success*, around which my marketing agency was created. This book goes deeper, providing the kind of detail that is meant to help Seller's navigate the Amazon platform without retaining a consultant. While success on Amazon is not as easy as it used to be, there are literally millions of Sellers on the online platform, growing every day. But the percentage of Sellers succeeding on Amazon is surprisingly low. Of the 2.7 million U.S. Sellers, for example, only

---

3   Scot Wingo, hosts "Amazon Q4 2019 Earnings Deep Dive." Jason & Scot Show (podcast), January 31, 2020, https://retailgeek.com/jason-scot-show-episode-206-amazon-earnings-q4-2020-deep-dive/.

6% (approx. 168,000) are generating sales of $100,000 a year or more, while fewer than 1.5% (approx. 40,000) are at $500,000 a year in sales.[4] As a former Amazon Top 200 Seller, I have the battle-scars and experience to help Sellers climb in the rankings and the humility to admit it's not that easy.

Being an Amazon Seller is hard, really hard, but together with my brothers, we found creative ways to adapt and, ultimately, thrive. But it wasn't until I met billion dollar brand-maker Rick Cesari that we reached the "next level," incorporating his merchandising magic into our *Seller's Survival Guide*. It was Rick who taught me how to put the customer at the center of every product decision—authentically. And it is here where we 3P Sellers have Amazon beat; where the little guy actually has the advantage.

While Amazon retail and 1P sellers are limited in the information they can share through product listings, 3P Sellers have greater freedom to create a strong presence beyond Amazon. I can't stress this enough. Rick and I both like to say that we're sales agnostic; that a sale is a sale, regardless of its point of origin. While listing your products on Amazon should be a fundamental feature of every product marketing plan, limiting yourself to Amazon hinders your chances of creating an enduring brand. Furthermore, your success *off* Amazon will enhance your performance *on* Amazon. In Chapter 10, Rick goes into great detail about the value of expanding your business off Amazon, with helpful tips from his favorite omni-channel approach to marketing.

Throughout this book, you'll learn more about the sizable opportunities available to Amazon Sellers, as well as reliable sales and marketing strategies designed to safeguard you from the digital quicksand. Rick and I will share our years of experience both on and off Amazon, with the goal of equipping you with the same knowledge and winning strategies

---

4   Marketplace Pulse Year in Review 2019. https://www.marketplacepulse.com/marketplaces-year-in-review-2019.

that helped us create brands and consistently grow sales for our clients. The Amazon Third-Party Seller is the lifeblood of Amazon.com and my dream, Mr. Bezos, is for 3P Sellers to have a meaningful seat at your table. Amazon would not exist as the retail e-commerce giant it is today without 3P Sellers, nor will Amazon have a bright future without them. The more that Amazon Sellers succeed today by doing things the right way for their customers, the more I believe my dream will come true.

Jason Boyce
Princeton, New Jersey

SECTION I

Amazon: Why and How

Chapter 1:

FROM NOWHERE TO *EVERYWHERE*

My journey on Amazon started in 2003, long before Jeff Bezos realized his vision of the *Everything Store* we know today. Amazon offered products in multiple categories, like books, electronics, even clothing, but it wasn't anything like it is now. After the dot-com bubble burst in 2001, Amazon was hurting and relied on a deal it struck with Toys "R" Us in August of 2000 (among other deals) to keep it alive. Under that agreement, Toys "R" Us paid $50 million a year for 10 years, plus a percentage of sales, for an exclusivity provision with exceptions that made them the sole seller of toys on Amazon.

But in 2002 Amazon started allowing other businesses to list their goods on the Amazon.com platform, including toys. I know, because in the holiday season of 2003, I was making daily trips in a U-Haul Truck to a Los Angeles distribution center to fill orders for the Razor Scooters I'd sold on Amazon the night before—thousands upon thousands of them. My brothers and I were selling the same scooter on Amazon that Toys "R" Us was selling, and we were *killing it!* Not surprisingly, Toys "R" Us was not pleased, and they later filed a lawsuit against Amazon that took them more than a decade to win. In the meantime, Amazon doubled in size and Toys "R" Us went bankrupt.

Not only was Amazon inviting greater competition among Sellers who were selling *to* Amazon, known as first-party sellers (1P), but Team Bezos had opened the door to Third-Party Sellers (3P), who sold products *on* Amazon. Saul Hansell, in an article for *The New York Times* explained Amazon's virtual surge as motivated by the desire "to replicate the success of eBay," whose first-of-its-kind digital auction-style format was kicking Amazon's butt.[5]

In 2003 we were one of the first to get a phone call from Amazon, back when desk telephones were still wired to the wall, about selling our basketball hoops in their brand new Sports & Outdoors category. At the time, the hoops, for which we were driving online traffic (at a nickel a click) were noticeably outperforming other hoops on search engines like Overture.com (later acquired by Yahoo). In fact, we were selling basketball hoops on Amazon.com *before* Amazon itself was selling basketball hoops on Amazon!

Of course we weren't the only ones being recruited to expand Amazon's stake in the virtual marketplace. Amazon was calling everyone with

---

5   Hansell, Saul. "Toys 'R' Us Sues Amazon.com Over Exclusive Sales Agreement." *The New York Times*, May 25, 2004.

an online presence. What began as an easy new sales channel for us pioneers quickly became harder as more sellers flocked to sell their wares on the new online marketplace. Back then, my brothers and I were selling other people's brands, a model that later became unsustainable for us on Amazon because every time a new Seller launched the same product, they'd do so at a lower price to win the sale. In response, we were forced to lower our prices and our profit margins began to shrink—fast. To compound the problem, Amazon itself got into the game, buying our same products from the same brands and selling them for less.

Spalding was a top-selling brand for us at the time. In fact, we sold so many Spalding basketball products online that Spalding gave us all-expense-paid trips to attend NBA All-Star games for four straight years in a row. The best part? We were booked into the same hotels as the NBA legends. I'll never forget telling Shaq in a hotel elevator how he broke my heart when he left Los Angeles for Miami! But as competition exploded on Amazon, boosted by the Prime Free 2-Day Shipping rollout in 2005, we went from owning the coveted Buy Box for most of Spalding's top-selling products to losing them all to Amazon, along with that all-expense-paid All-Star experience. Oh well, thanks for the memories.

We knew this would happen eventually, but we were shocked by how quickly Amazon bought and resold every brand imaginable. They had the traffic data, product data, sales data, and knowledge from 3P Sellers like us to literally take over entire categories—overnight. Add to it the tremendous buying power of Amazon; then subtract out the small guys' ability to compete. The only way to maintain our sales and stay in the Buy Box was to lower prices. This *race to the bottom* became an inevitable consequence of Amazon's Marketplace structure, and it was no doubt part of Mr. Bezos' original vision to have the lowest prices, no matter what. This phenomenon still vexes Sellers today, and it eventually forced my brothers and me to rethink our entire approach to selling online. This process repeated itself four times over the years until we finally landed on the strategy that I will share with you in the coming chapters.

IT'S BIGGER THAN YOU THINK

Amazon is everywhere. It is on a speedy trajectory to become the largest retailer in the United States as it continues to gain on Walmart. Nearly half of the U.S. e-commerce market share already belongs to Amazon, with eBay, once the dominant leader in the field, in a distant second position with just 6.6% of online market share.[6]

Top 10 U.S. companies based on % of e-commerce sales

1. Amazon	49.1%
2. eBay	6.6%
3. Apple	3.9%
4. Walmart	3.7%
5. The Home Depot	1.5%
6. Best Buy	1.3%
7. QVC Group	1.2%
8. Macy's	1.2%
9. Costco	1.2%
10. Wayfair	1.1%

Source: eMarketer, July 2018

6   Ingrid Lunden, "Amazon's share of the US e-commerce market is now 49%, or 5% of all retail spend," TechCrunch. July 13, 2018. https://techcrunch. com/2018/07/13/amazons-share-of-the-us-e-commerce-market-is-now-49-or-5- of-all-retail-spend/.

Ironically, in 2019 eMarketer revised this initial 49% market share estimate down to 38% following a vague comment Bezos made in his annual shareholder letter. In it he said that 58% of its e-commerce sales come from Third Party Sellers. This downward revision from such a closely followed researcher highlights a glowing problem. No one really knows how many retail sales go through Amazon.com. Only Amazon knows, and they aren't sharing that information despite the fact that they are a publicly-traded company. Additionally, DigitalCommerce 360 reported $602 billion in 2019 online sales[7] and MarketplacePulse estimated that Amazon's Gross Merchandise Value was $335 billion.[8] If these numbers are accurate, then it is clear that Amazon has increased its market share to 55%, well beyond the 2018 market share estimate. I didn't buy what eMarketer was selling when they decreased their estimate, but one thing is clear: Amazon wants to appear a lot smaller than they actually are, especially as the trustbusters gather at their gate.

Either way, when you look at Amazon's reported sales, it's easy to see how big they are. But consider this: they're even bigger than what's being reported. Amazon does not disclose the full retail value of goods sold on its platform, known as the Gross Merchandise Value (GMV) because more than half of its sales come from Third-Party Sellers, for which Amazon must only report the fees it charges them. If I sell a $100 chair on Amazon as a 3P Seller, for example, Amazon will charge me a $15 seller fee for the right to sell my product on their website. While I must report the full $100 GMV to the IRS, Amazon need only report the $15 fee, typically 15% of GMV. With 58% of Amazon sales coming from Third-Party Sellers, the sum value of what's *not* being reported by Amazon is staggering. Estimates range in 2020 from $330

7   Jessica Young, "US ecommerce sales grow 14.9% in 2019." Digital Commerce 360. February 19, 2020. https://www.digitalcommerce360.com/article/us-ecommerce-sales/

8   Marketplace Pulse, "Amazon GMV in 2019," February 4, 2020. https://www.marketplacepulse.com/articles/amazon-gmv-in-2019

billion[9] to as high as $530 billion,[10] which already makes them larger than Walmart. Just sayin'.

Amazon has been so successful and so dominant that the U.S. and European Union governments may be the only overseers with the power to slow the company's upward trajectory. Mr. Bezos's empire has a slew of detractors calling for, among other things, increased taxes on the business and, in the most extreme case, a full-blown breakup. Even if Amazon were to be brought to heel, its competitors would likely still be outrun by the Amazon equivalent of the Baby Bells, a reference to the U.S. regional telephone companies that were formed from the breakup of AT&T ("Ma Bell") in the mid-1980s. Third-Party Sellers already sell more on Amazon than Amazon sells on its own platform, and a breakup would move Amazon.com from the #1 largest e-commerce website to the #1 *and* #2 largest e-commerce websites. I know a lot of 3P Sellers who would welcome the thought of not competing against Amazon on their Marketplace, but who knows what might happen if Amazon Retail has its own website and is forced to compete? We're likely some years away from knowing how the current antitrust inquiries play out, but until then, Amazon will continue devouring the competition; of that, you can be certain.

IF YOU'RE NOT ON AMAZON, YOU'RE NOT ONLINE.

I tell my clients, if you're not on Amazon, your product isn't really online. It's a slight exaggeration, but I'm convinced that being on Amazon has become a necessity in today's retail environment because Amazon has literally become *The Internet of Products*. Why? A major reason is that consumers don't have to start on Amazon.com to wind up there. The company's tentacles spread throughout the entire internet, and it is tough to avoid them. Forty-seven percent (47%) of people searching for a product to buy start their search

9   Marketplace Pulse, ibid.
10   Scot Wingo, hosts "Amazon Q4 2019 Earnings Deep Dive." Jason & Scot Show (podcast), January 31, 2020, https://retailgeek.com/jason-scot-show-episode-206-amazon-earnings-q4-2020-deep-dive/.

on Amazon.com compared to 35% who use Google.[11] And that's not even the most amazing part. Because of Amazon's long internet history and its massive online presence, search engines like Google and Bing give Amazon prime digital real estate on their Search Results Pages (SRPs). As a result, Amazon not only enjoys millions of unpaid organic search results links, but it also pays for clicks on those same search engines and comparison shopping engines (like Shopzilla and Pricegrabber) for top-ranking product search results. If all product searches lead to Amazon (and most do), then that's where you need to be to sell your products. Simple as that.

The Google Search Results Page (SRP) pictured below demonstrates my point. In this scenario, a shopper enters two words into the Google search field: "water flask." In return, several rows of information are displayed, starting with Google's Product Listing Ads (PLAs). The pay-per-click PLA program gives priority position to products for which retailers have paid top dollar to drive traffic to their websites. In this case, Amazon has two products featured, the Hydro Flask and S'well bottles. Google AdWords Ads are displayed next, both with links to Amazon. Additionally, and as a result of Amazon's page-rank power, Amazon products also top the free organic search results, with links back to their website. Of the nine product links for this SRP, Amazon owns five of them. Wait a minute. Is this Google or Amazon? *(see image on next page)*

Amazon also has millions of affiliate publishers, digital display banners (virtual billboards), review sites, and a dozen new media stories each week, all driving traffic to their platform. When it comes to consumers searching for a product to buy, Amazon has it locked down. Amazon.com has always been about selling you products and making that purchase as frictionless as possible. Every update or iteration since its inception has cleared the buyer's path of roadblocks. Their entire e-commerce ecosystem is built around making the path to purchase as smooth and fast as

11 Krista Garcia, "More Product Searches Start on Amazon: Google is losing its grip on valuable search data." *eMarketer*, September 7, 2018, https://www.emarketer.com/content/more-product-searches-start-on-amazon.

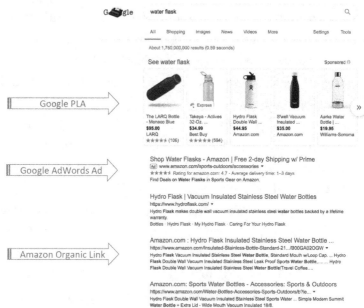

possible, and no other competitor comes close to matching that experience. How do they do it?

Thirty years of purchasing data gives Amazon a tremendous advantage—especially because they are competing on their own platform against Sellers who don't have access to the same information. They've been able to translate decades of Seller data into a delivery system that is custom-fit for their customer, or any customer for that matter. As a result, Amazon enjoys a much higher purchase intent than other e-commerce retailers. It's not unusual for conversion rates to go as high as 25% on Amazon, for example, while other e-commerce sites are typically thrilled to see rates of 2 to 3%. The folks at Amazon Advertising put it best when they said that Facebook knows what you like, Google knows what you search, but Amazon knows what you buy! To further this point, Amazon Sponsored Brands, formerly known as Headline Ads, get 42% more clicks and 3.5 times the conversions compared to Google PLA Ads.[12] I

12   Nivedya Varma. "Amazon Versus Google Search: Who is Winning the Battle and How?" MarTechSeries, July 30, 2018.

see these numbers every day when assessing data for my clients. Amazon has stopped at nothing to satisfy its customers. In return, their customers are more comfortable buying their products on Amazon than from any other online retailer.

SUCCESS IN THE MARGINS

As formidable a competitor as Amazon is, with a greater number of products online than there are people in the United States, don't let their dominance discourage you from listing your products on their platform. Here's why. Of the 2.7 million U.S. Amazon Sellers, fewer than 7% are producing $100,000 or more in annual sales; which means 93% are treading water.

Distribution of Amazon Sellers by Annual Sales

Instead of thrashing around with the bottom millions, hold your own against the Top Sellers by using strategies like ours to get to (and stay) on top. For nearly two decades, I have invested tens of thousands of hours picking and developing products to sell on Amazon. I have also created cool brands, all while negotiating an online platform that aims to eat me for lunch. The fierceness of this experience forced me to develop a battle-tested plan that has kept me in the game.

When I look back on the distance my brothers and I traveled on Amazon since we launched our first products in 2003, it honestly feels like we orbited the sun—with the scorch marks to prove it! Countless algorithm changes, platform updates, policy tweaks, and Buy Box refinements created a mess of headaches (and heartaches) over the years, while also teaching us to be responsive and poised for change. Hackers, counterfeiters, tricksters, and Amazon itself soured us at times, but they also hardened us to the realities of this savage landscape. As we navigated this unique ecosystem, we learned that the best way to survive was by following a motto I learned as a Marine: *Improvise, Adapt, Overcome.*

Graduating from the Amazon School of Hard Knocks, like boot camp, gave me the raw experience and fortitude necessary to succeed on the retail platform. It also forced me to work smart and create a process that is repeatable and dependable—even on a platform that is unpredictable and often contrary. Amazon is not for everybody. I get asked all the time about what it takes to become a Top Seller, and as much as I like to quantify stuff, defining the characteristics of the hundreds of Top Sellers I've met over the years is really tough. That said, I'm always on the lookout for patterns, and it's hard to ignore some of the most recognizable traits of the people I've come to admire, both for their achievements and for the ways in which they've persevered on Amazon.

5 COMMON TRAITS OF AMAZON TOP SELLERS

1. They run the marathon; not the sprint
2. They don't sweat the small stuff (and they press on)
3. They have a sense of style and they use it to build a great brand
4. They value metrics and enjoy tracking them (ad nauseam)
5. They are lifelong learners, who simply must keep learning to survive

OWN YOUR DESTINY

While hard work and perseverance are among the qualities of the Amazon Top Sellers I've known, it takes a whole lot more to be successful in today's virtual marketplace. The sheer volume of competition, coupled with Amazon's price-squeezing tactics, make it nearly impossible to prevail on attitude alone. Remember at the top of this chapter I said that the pace of growth at Amazon forced my brothers and me to rethink our entire approach to selling online? It's true. Once Amazon started buying our products and selling them for less, all bets were off. The tireless work ethic we brought to the platform in 2003 was no longer enough to keep us on top.

Over the next decade, I concentrated on developing a winning formula. We wanted to do better than just make ends meet on Amazon, and with thousands of competitors pouring onto the platform every day, we knew we had to establish a reliable game plan. I became obsessed with our performance data, making incremental adjustments to every aspect of our selling and marketing processes, and measuring the results. Ironically, Amazon's own customer feedback tools and limited metrics would come to feature prominently in my *Seller's Survival Guide*. But the most dependable tactic? Branding. Today's Third-Party Seller has the unique advantage of shaping their brand message and controlling the narrative about their products and services—far more than Amazon Retail and its 1P sellers. Brand-building is one area where Amazon and its minions fall short, and the steps for building an enduring twenty-first century brand are an integral part of what was to become *The Amazon Jungle Seller's Survival Guide*. While my brothers and I understood how to create a cool brand, having created several of our own, it wasn't until I met Rick Cesari, the pioneer of direct response television marketing, that my survival guide got a major upgrade.

I still remember like it was yesterday, sitting in the audience of an opening conference session led by Rick. It was the 2016 Prosper Show for Amazon Sellers, where thousands of Third-Party Sellers have access to dozens of leading solutions and industry experts, like Rick. In his captivating keynote presentation, Rick made a simple point, the gravity of which nearly floored me at the time: *features tell, but benefits sell.* Now Rick didn't originate the phrase, but in the examples he shared with us that day, working with products like The Juiceman, Sonicare,

OxiClean, and GoPro, Rick profoundly altered the way I marketed products going forward.

I mentioned in the introduction that I introduced myself to Rick after that presentation, where we discovered we lived in neighboring towns just east of Seattle. Our proximity nurtured a mutual friendship and weekly coffee meetings, where we exchanged strategies to boost sales and build brands. We made a deal that I would teach him everything I knew about Amazon, and he would teach me everything he knew about building great brands. It was Rick who urged me to launch my own marketing agency, and he who gave me the confidence to guide other Amazon Sellers in following the same proven formula that worked so well for me and my brothers. Additionally, I now had Rick's direct response marketing lessons to add to my survival guide, with first-hand experience in what a difference that makes!

After meeting Rick at the conference, my brothers and I applied what we learned about highlighting a product's benefits over its features. We changed our Product Detail Pages to tout the lifestyle advantages of our air hockey tables, for example, like bringing friends and family together, instead of focusing on the size of the blower. Within a week we saw a 400% increase in engagement on our website and a 25% jump in sales. We were no longer selling a sturdy table with a high-end blower. We were helping families make memories!

In the following chapters, we'll walk you through the fundamental steps for finding and listing a winning product, drawing on the combined expertise and experience of a battle-tested Amazon Seller and a Product Whisperer. *The Amazon Jungle Seller's Survival Guide* that Rick and I have crafted together here will put you in a position to own your own destiny as an Amazon Top Seller. More importantly, you'll have the skillset for building an enduring brand, on and off the Amazon.com platform.

Building a twenty-first century brand requires you to authentically tell your customer *why you* chose the product you're selling and *how their* lives will be changed for the better when they buy it. In the next chapter, I share my personal story and how it followed an unlikely path to Top-Seller status. Later we'll share tips for writing your own back story. In Chapter 3, I'll help you determine whether there's a suitable market for your product and how to make your product stand out in a crowd. In Section II, "Let's Get Started," you'll learn how to get your product made, plus foundational steps for getting your product listed for search and for sales whether you are new to Amazon or already have listings. In chapters 6 and 7, we'll show you how Top Sellers consistently optimize their listings using the same Direct-To-Consumer (DTC) marketing tactics that helped Rick create so many enduring brands. In the final chapters of the book, we'll focus on expanding your business on and off Amazon, and I'll talk specifically about the role Amazon Ads play in fortifying your Amazon business. As I mentioned earlier, listing your products on Amazon is a fundamental feature of every product marketing plan, but limiting yourself to Amazon limits your chances of creating a brand that will thrive. In Chapter 10, Rick talks about the value of expanding your business and building your brand off Amazon, with recommended strategies from his omnichannel approach to marketing.

There is a lot of information out there about how to make your fortune on Amazon, but being successful online requires more than a mechanical list of steps for listing your products on Amazon. In these pages, Rick and I have tried to capture our combined 50+ years of selling and marketing experience and boil it down to the human element, because *what matters* to your customer *is what sells*. And it all begins with what matters most to you.

CHAPTER SUMMARY

- The Amazon.com platform has dramatically evolved over three decades and has permanently reshaped retail.
- If you're not on Amazon, you're not online.
- More people go to Amazon to search for products than they go to online search engines, like Google or Bing.
- More than half of all Sellers on Amazon are Third-Party Sellers.
- While there are 5 million Sellers on Amazon, fewer than 5% (200,000 Sellers) are generating $100,000 or more in annual sales.
- There is an untapped opportunity for a small group of Sellers.
- There are common characteristics among Top Sellers, including persistence and resilience, but it takes something more than sheer grit to build a lasting presence on the Amazon.com platform.
- Third-Party Sellers have a competitive edge on Amazon. The authors' combined 50+ years of experience on and off the Amazon.com platform will show you how to exploit that advantage using the same customer-centric, direct response strategies that launched billion dollar brands like GoPro, George Foreman Grill, and Oxiclean, among others.

Chapter 2:

START WITH *YOUR* STORY

"I HAVE ALWAYS BELIEVED THAT WHATEVER GOOD
OR BAD FORTUNE MAY COME OUR WAY WE CAN
ALWAYS GIVE IT MEANING AND TRANSFORM IT
INTO SOMETHING OF VALUE."

SIDDHARTHA, BY HERMAN HESSE

Your story is the foundation for how others understand you and what you have to offer. It's about connecting a human face and experience to the products or services you are selling. Presenting yourself not as just a company, but as a person with goals, a heartbeat and a mission helps foster trust and lays the groundwork for an enduring brand. As much as I know that's true, and I always advise my clients to start with their story, I was reluctant to share mine for this book. Rick had to convince me to do it—repeatedly. In the process of sharing our origin story, we must necessarily relive the experience, something I was trying to avoid, primarily because my experience as a Seller got launched unconventionally. Yet the passion and conviction with which I ultimately created enduring brands and became a Top 200 Seller came straight from the lessons learned on that journey. Telling it reminded me of that.

A DOWNWARD SPIRAL

There was a time a while back when I could not have imagined myself being successful. For a dismal period in my early twenties, just getting out of bed before the next party was a major accomplishment. I didn't like myself then, and it eventually took the kind act of a stranger to awaken me to a new way of being. High school started out well enough. I excelled in sports and in the classroom. I had high hopes of getting a scholarship and becoming the first member of my family to graduate from college. Like most high school athletes, I also dreamed of playing in college. But no matter how good I got at any one of the three sports I played, I would always do something stupid to sabotage my progress. There was something holding me back, and it really got me down. That's when I started drinking.

I clearly remember the first time I had a drink. It was like a million lights went off in my brain and I knew that I had to have more. I went from not drinking to drinking every day. I even got drunk before a varsity basketball game. It wasn't my proudest moment, but drinking became part of who I was and how I navigated the world. Despite my alcohol addiction, my grades and sports got me into Pepperdine University—the proudest moment of my life to that point. A kid from the small cow town of Hanford, California was going to be the first member of his family to graduate from college! I was on cloud nine; at least for a short while.

Although I started college with such high hopes, trouble followed me in new ways. I was really struggling to keep up with my studies. I've always had an insatiable appetite for learning, and I wanted desperately to be able to devour my new lessons, but the reading assignments were proving too difficult. It took an almost Herculean effort for me to get through one book, and the hardship was taking a physical toll. Headaches and exhaustion were my new norm, something I'd experienced in high school, but to a lesser degree. I fell behind in my studies and failed my first round of midterms. I was carrying the pressure of generations of family before me to be the very first to graduate from college, and I was failing. What I didn't fail at was drinking, and I took that skill to a whole new level in Malibu. I still remember seeing a certain "Brat Pack" actor snort lines of cocaine off of a kitchen table at a party. It was exactly the wrong remedy for what was holding me back. Not surprisingly, I was quietly asked by the dean to seek a college education elsewhere. Ouch.

THE GOOD DOCTOR

The Law of Serendipity states that the Universe bends in our direction by providing us with seemingly accidental circumstances that we call good luck. On the day I was approached by a total stranger while trying to score some cheap booze, I felt the full force of this effect. I was standing in the beer aisle inside Gelson's supermarket in Los Angeles looking for the cheapest way to keep my buzz on when a man approached me. He looked at me with compassionate eyes and asked me what I was doing to myself. I was so stunned by his candor that it took me a moment to respond with something like, "What are you talking about, man? I'm doing just fine." It was as if he was responding to a silent call for help I hadn't realized I was broadcasting. Next, he told me to stop punishing myself and to show up at his house later that Friday evening for dinner with his family. I was too astonished to decline the offer.

Every Friday night, Barbara and Ken ("Dr. K") Klaristenfeld and family totally unplug. Starting sundown Friday through sundown Saturday, no television, no video games, and no electronics. Just a family dinner, where Barb and Ken's four boys would stand up one at a time and thank their mother for at least one thing she'd done for them during the week. They would then bow their heads and receive a blessing from their father. Frankly, I was dumbstruck by the grace and compassion with which this family connected. I'm pretty sure I didn't say anything through the entire meal, but I can recall the experience of nearly 30 years ago like it was yesterday, and it still makes me choke up. One of the oddest things about the experience, as foreign as it was to me, was that I felt like I'd come home.

What followed after dinner was equally unexpected and would later spark the idea of a family business the Klaristenfeld brothers and I would start together and expand on Amazon a decade later. After dinner, the K's played games like cribbage, table tennis, foosball, and basketball. If it wasn't electronic, we played it. I was so moved by the entire Friday night experience, that I just kept coming over, every Friday that followed, until I was unofficially adopted as the fifth brother.

Several months after our first meeting at Gelson's, I moved in to their home. Getting to know Dr. and Mrs. K better led to difficult conversations about my past and ultimately to the discovery of a learning disability, which helped explain my troubles at Pepperdine. They arranged for treatment that made it possible for me to return to college, where I was finally able to read and learn without physical pain or fatigue. I started first at a junior college, where I relearned the fundamentals; then I transferred to California State University, Northridge, where I earned a business degree.

A different conversation with the good doctor uncovered something else about my past that I'd buried so deeply I had to question whether it happened at all. One afternoon after school, I was explaining to him how my life had started out great, with a happy, healthy family and two younger sisters I adored. He interrupted me because I'd only ever mentioned one sister, Shawna. It took me a minute to sort out an avalanche of memories and emotions, but then the facts came back like hammer blows.

It was eight days before my seventh birthday. My baby sister, Mandy, wandered out of a side door and into the driveway at the exact moment my father was backing out of the garage in his Ford Bronco. I was in the passenger seat when Mandy was struck. She was killed instantly.

Even greater than the pain of losing my sister was seeing my dad in despair. I was there, next to him, when it happened. I knew it wasn't his fault, and I quickly fabricated a story to try to take away his guilt and pain. I told him I had left the door open; that it was my fault Mandy got out. But nothing would console him. For more than 20 years, my family never mentioned Mandy or the accident, yet I had internalized the blame and lived with this dark secret until it surfaced at the Klaristenfeld's. After countless more conversations with Dr. K, I realized that the accident was not my fault. In fact, I later learned that Mandy had used a stool to unlock and open the door so that she could get out and play with us. Knowing this helped me stop punishing myself for this terrible calamity and accept it for the horrible accident it was. Soon afterward, everything became clearer to me. I also stopped drinking.

I don't know what was more difficult, overcoming my learning disabilities, remembering those painful childhood memories, or quitting my addiction. They were all battles worth fighting and I never would have been able to beat them without the loving kindness of a stranger at Gelson's. Dr. K helped me regain the joy of learning, helped me stop sabotaging myself, and he made it possible for me to live the life I live today, with a beautiful family and two happy, healthy daughters of my own.

A few weeks before graduation from CSU, Northridge, I came across a Marine Lt. Colonel in his dress blue uniform on the cover of *Inc. Magazine*. The title of the article inside read, "The Best MBA Program in America." I wanted to be a leader, and the Marines provided just the opportunity and training I was looking for. So much of what I learned as a Marine Officer has served me well in life, in business, and as an Amazon Seller. Marines lead from the front and by example. Excuses have no place in the United States Marine Corps, and the worst decision a leader can make is to not make one at all. I learned that planning and preparation provide structure and purpose, along with flexibility and responsiveness, because once you cross the line of departure, everything changes. The same goes for selling on Amazon.

INSTRUCTIONS: PLAY.

After four years in the USMC, I was about to accept an offer to join the Corps' elite Fleet Antiterrorism Security Team, or FAST Company, when Harvey Klaristenfeld, Dr. K's older brother, died suddenly. "Uncle Harvey" was a larger than life businessman, who'd made and lost half a dozen fortunes in the Big Apple. My brothers and I idolized him. On that cold afternoon in Manhattan, while his wife and two young children laid Harvey to rest, I knew that my time as a Marine was over. Harvey's funeral helped me realize the one thing I wanted more than anything in the world, a family. I knew that if I joined FAST Company, I may never have that chance. So I made my decision right then, at the edge of a burial site, to leave the Corps and take a page from Uncle Harvey's book: I would start my own business.

A few days later I was back at the K's family dinner table brainstorming with my brothers about next steps. It was Ari's idea to start an e-commerce website selling basketball hoops. He even gave it a name: Superduperhoops.com and, later, Superdupergames.com. Our pledge was to create a brand of products that reflected our family values; merchandise that would bring friends and family together. Our mission was simple. *Instructions: Play.* At the time, there were only a few other online sellers in our categories, and after our youngest brother, Josh, coded the first website (in his free time after school), we grew quickly—from $100,000 in 2002 to $1 million in 2003. That's when Amazon called.

Rick loves this story of how I turned my life around and how family played a central role in my healing, as well as in the brands my brothers and I first launched on Amazon. A pioneer of direct response advertising and master story-teller, Rick taught me that each and every product has a unique story that should be heard. Products like GoPro and George Foreman Grill are widely known because Rick tapped into the customers' experience with these products, and he shared those stories with the world. In Chapter 7, Rick offers some of his direct response strategies for launching new products, as well as case studies from clients who bloomed after using them. Bottom line? You've got to *ask good questions* and *you must listen*. Rick is a great listener, and his ability to connect with his clients' origin stories allowed him to see exactly what was needed to make a hit, time and time again.

Over the course of nearly two decades on Amazon, my brothers and I reinvented our selling strategy a dozen times to keep pace with the onslaught of policy changes, growth, and upgrades to the platform. One thing that never changed? Our commitment to our brand story. The big question in today's market environment is: *How do you set your product apart so that when people think of that product they choose yours?* Getting people to choose *you* requires brand trust. Intuitively, my brothers and I seemed to understand this, but working with Rick confirmed our belief that every brand has an origin story and a purpose for being. Telling *that* story helps establish an authentic connection with consumers and sets in motion a critical feedback loop by which you can improve your products and deepen a sense of loyalty to your brand. Tell this story often because doing so will help you improve it and tighten it over time. Then place it on your brand's website, as well as your Amazon Brand Store, about which you'll learn more shortly.

Once you've established your authentic backstory, you're ready to sell. Maybe you already have products listed on Amazon? Do they reflect your story's mission? Are they the right products for your brand? Whether you're already selling on Amazon or only just thinking about it, selecting products with winning potential is a critical next step. In Chapter 3, I will walk you through my tested method for identifying winning products and show you how to assess the market potential for the products you've selected. The number of products and Sellers on Amazon.com can literally make your head spin, and these numbers are growing every day. By knowing where to look, and by using existing customer feedback, you can identify opportunity. If there's one thing I've learned that holds true over time, it's this: *If you know what you are doing, no matter how big Amazon gets, there is always opportunity*. In the next chapter, I'll show you where to look.

CHAPTER SUMMARY

- Presenting yourself not just as a company, but as a person with goals and a mission helps foster trust and lays the groundwork for an enduring brand.

- Sharing a deeply personal story is hard sometimes, but it is often the backbone of your success on (and off) Amazon. Authenticity is key. You can't fake your story.

- Direct response advertising pioneer Rick Cesari is a master storyteller, who taught me that each and every product has a story to tell. Products like GoPro and George Foreman Grill are household names because Rick used his marketing knowledge to harvest customers' experiences and share those stories broadly.

- When your products are connected to your origin story, it gives meaning to something that is otherwise impersonal.

- Telling your story builds relationships and inspires your customers to make decisions beyond pure logical calculations.

- Share your story broadly. It is your connection to your customer base and the foundation for your brand.

Chapter 3:

RESEARCH. THE KEY TO WINNING ON AMAZON

"KNOW YOUR MARKET
AND LET YOUR MARKET KNOW YOU."

SAI VENU GOPAL MOULI

T he single most important element of long-term success on Amazon
is finding a great product to sell on their platform. But how? Con-
veniently, Amazon.com is one of the best places to conduct product
research, with automated tools in place to help you size up the competition; plus a built-in feedback loop to let you know how people feel about
what's already out there. I shake my head when I read how Amazon is the
place to be if you want to *make an easy million dollars.* That's just not how
it works. Amazon is not a get-rich-quick scheme. At least not anymore!
Like any other sales success story, in any other marketing channel, you've
got to have a great product *and* there's got to be a market for it.

One of the advantages of having sold thousands of products on Amazon over the years is learning to recognize the consistent, repeatable patterns that exist there while the rest of the Amazon.com platform evolves into something different every day. Identifying these repeatable patterns, and using them to my advantage, led me to become an Amazon Top 200 Seller. Today this experience helps me guide clients towards success with their products, whether they are new to Amazon or have been selling on the platform for many years.

I should also explain that there are plenty of Sellers who've had terrific financial success cherry-picking top products from dozens of unrelated product categories and slapping their brand name on them. This can be a profitable strategy, but I don't believe it is a good way to build a lasting brand. It's also not my style. Perhaps the biggest lesson I learned early on Amazon is the power of an enduring brand. It's where you can really separate yourself from the competition and build a loyal customer base on and off the platform.

Over the next several pages, I'll walk you through my tested method for finding great products and measuring their sales potential on Amazon. I will also demonstrate how to use available tools, with help from some easily downloadable software, to ensure the investment is well worth your time. We'll also look at my favorite pastime—taking products that are flawed, but for which there is a market, and making them shine. It's often these "ugly ducklings" that provide the greatest margins for success on Amazon. I'll show you how to spot them and how to transform an ugly gizmo into an overnight swan.

5 ESSENTIAL STEPS FOR FINDING A WINNING PRODUCT

1. Find a product that moves you
2. Be certain there is a market for your product
3. Test to see if the market is big enough
4. Find flaws. It's where the opportunity is.

5. Hit the sweet spot

STEP 1: WHAT MOVES YOU?

If you lack enthusiasm for the products you sell, you will alienate your customer in one way or another. To put it more positively, having passion for what and how you're selling is key to making your customer (and yourself) happy. If you're already selling on Amazon, how do your current products make you feel? Are you proud of them? Do you love sharing how great they are with your friends and family? If not, then maybe it's time for an upgrade, or maybe it's even time to try a new line of products. The connection doesn't have to be profound. If you're just starting out, perhaps you bought a product that you believe, with a few minor changes, could be really special. Think about it. How many times have you purchased a product that you were really excited about only to be let down? Could *you* do better?

One of my favorite examples comes from the talented founders of the travel accessories brand mumi, whose award-winning designs grew out of their own real-life experience. Gabriela Mekler and Maribel Moreno discovered their inspiration while traveling abroad, where the suitcases they took with them fell short of their needs and their impeccable sense of style. There were too few options for keeping their belongings organized. When they searched for packing cubes to better organize their belongings, they found them to be really boring and uninspiring. Besides being dull, the stuff that was out there was generally flimsy and lacked function. Mekler and Moreno were so frustrated by the limited options that they decided to take matters into their own hands. The result? They turned their passion into a thriving new brand, with a loyal following of customers who can, thanks to mumi, better organize their lives on and off the road. I especially love their tagline: *be mumi, be happy.* And every new design they present honestly makes me feel that way.

Once you've found your inspiration, the next step is to find out if Amazon customers are buying the same or similar items. Sizing up the market for new and existing products is one of my favorite parts of selling on Amazon. It combines using some of the analytical tools that are already out there, along with your own creative intuition. Feeling good about a product is a critical first step, but now you're ready to put it to the test.

STEP 2: WHAT'S HOT?

To underscore the importance of choosing a product that people care about (and one for which there is an existing market), I'll share a story about a new product idea I had some years ago. It was a line of folding leg foosball and air hockey tables, and I was absolutely certain they would take the home recreation market by storm. Can't you just picture it? Fold up the table when you're done with the game, then reclaim the space in your basement or den. Great idea, right? Shortly after landing an ocean container full of my bright idea, it was clear I had a problem. The tables sat in the warehouse, and they sat and sat. When they finally (and barely) started to sell, I discovered we had an even bigger issue: The legs didn't fold completely flat, making it impossible to slide the table under a bed! What a disaster (and a very expensive education). The experience taught me to first make sure there is a market for my "bright ideas" *before* investing cash in developing them. I also learned that I needed better sourcing and quality control procedures, something we'll explore in more detail in Chapter 4.

Only Steve Jobs could predict what customers wanted before they knew it for themselves. Hello, iPhone! The folding-leg folly taught me the hard way that I was no Steve Jobs, something my brothers still remind me about at the family dinner table. You may well be the next iconic innovator, but if you're merely human like me, then there are reliable steps you can take to measure the potential of a product *before* you pull the trigger.

And, somewhat ironically, Amazon is the best place to find out how other Sellers are performing in a targeted category. For nearly 20 years, I've used this same method to find my next great product. I now use this same method to calculate product potential for my clients. As you'll discover, you just have to know where to look.

When I was approached recently by a private equity firm in New York City looking to purchase a bird feeder business, I was excited to help out. They asked me to look at the company's current Amazon business as well as to identify areas for potential growth post-acquisition. Even though I'd never in my life searched for or shopped for bird feeders, I knew that my proven process would answer their questions, quickly. There are four steps I use to assess the market for any product before I go any further. I'll walk you through them using the bird feeder example.

4 Easy Steps for Market Assessment: A Bird Feeder Case Study
First, I begin by **searching the current brand's product(s) on Amazon**, in this case: bird feeders. This particular bird feeder had special suction cups and was made of acrylic so that it could be attached to the outside of your home window. Once loaded with birdseed, homeowners would enjoy a close-up view of all sorts of birds from the comfort of their home. What a great idea! I can't share their sales information, but I was surprised by the large number of units being sold each month. This was a sizable, respectable business.

Second, I **use web-based research software** that can be downloaded as a Chrome browser extension, and it will show the estimated monthly sales quantity of each item on an Amazon search results page. My favorite is Jungle Scout, and with its Chrome extension I was able to confirm the monthly sales estimates provided by the private equity firm. The company's bird feeder was doing really well. But the firm already knew that, and that's not why they were paying me. They wanted new opportunities.

Third, after I've confirmed the market performance of the existing product, I **scroll down the Product Detail Page (PDP) on Amazon**. The PDP is where a customer discovers the specific product details, including features, benefits, images, and price. To look for new product ideas for my client, I went to the PDP for the bird feeder they were investigating. I scrolled down the page until I found the Amazon Best Seller Rank (BSR) link with the subcategory name Birdhouses. The products I was investigating were ranked #1 for feeders and birdhouses. So how could I help them grow?

I did another Amazon Search for bird feeders, and I ran my Jungle Scout Chrome browser extension to see how other types of feeders were performing. I found several generating more in monthly sales than my client's top-seller. But how could that be, if ours was ranked on top? I clicked on the feeder with the larger sales volume and scrolled down to view its BSR. That's when I realized there were more than two bird feeder subcategories! This new subcategory was called Wild Bird Feeders, and the BSRs in this subcategory were outperforming the bird feeders in the Bird Feeders category. Jackpot! Now I knew how to increase, perhaps even double my client's revenue, with just one new product, and it would fit beautifully within their brand. The difference? My client's bird feeder was built for birdseed, whereas the other had top-sellers for hummingbird feeders with liquid feed. My client had an inviting and unique brand, with a distinctive birdseed feeder design. If they could engineer a product for hummingbirds, with similar design features to their original, then they'd likely double the size of their business overnight.

For the fourth and final step in my research, I shift to looking at the product reviews for competing products and I read *every bad review* for *every top-selling hummingbird feeder*. Across the spectrum I discovered some very interesting similarities. The biggest complaint? Hornets were getting through the holes in the feeder and they were stealing the food. Also, the products leaked and spilled feed. Some of the feeders were hard to fill. What if my client could address these issues in the form of a better design? The client loved the idea, and is now working on bringing a new kind of hummingbird feeder to the market. So long as they stay true to their brand and solve the issues raised by Amazon customers, then I'm confident the new feeder will be a hit.

This story about bird feeders offers a summary of how my research process works for people who are already selling on Amazon with an established brand. But they work just as effectively for new Sellers— someone, perhaps, with a passion for birdwatching and a creative design idea for making a better feeder. This reliable step-by-step process works wherever you are in the exploration process, whether you are a first-time Seller or looking to grow your Amazon business.

STEP 3: MARKET SIZE MATTERS!

Finding out the sales potential for your product makes smart business sense. It can also save you time and money, whether you are new to Amazon or trying to improve the results of your existing products on the platform. Do you remember my not-so-brilliant idea of introducing folding leg game tables into the market? Had I first investigated the market size for such an invention, I'd have learned it didn't exist, and I could have saved myself from making a six-figure mistake (and a lot of embarrassment at the family dinner table). You want to make sure the product you make is well-liked *and* is being purchased by Amazon customers. If you want to create a new product in a new market, then Rick can help you create a direct response TV campaign to educate the public; but Amazon, in my experience, isn't where you want to create the market.

I mentioned earlier how I used web-based research software to learn which products were ranked higher than others. That software simply replicates a method my brothers and I were using called the 999 Cart Trick, long before SaaS software companies like Jungle Scout and Helium10 were around. If you want to save the software fees, the cart trick is a great place to start. Without the software, it's quite a laborious process, checking multiple competitors across multiple categories, but the "intel" is critical and getting to it manually is a good exercise in understanding what you're measuring. Here's how it's done:

The 999 Cart Trick
1. Find a competitive product to research
2. Add the item to the Amazon cart
3. Increase the quantity to 999

If 999 products are not available, a message will appear showing you the total number of units available. By tracking the available quantity each day for seven days, you can calculate how many units are being sold daily. For example, if there are 20 products on Day 1, 18 on Day 2, and 15 on Day 3 (up to Day 7), you can estimate they are selling between two and three products a day. Once you have a daily average, you can generate a monthly average. And, Voila! You now have a reliable estimate for how much your competitor is selling on Amazon. It's important to note that the monthly sales estimates may not hold throughout the year, especially for seasonal products. Snow shoes, for example, will move more units in January than in July.

STEP 4: FIND FLAWS. IT'S WHERE THE OPPORTUNITY IS.

I've always felt that the best way to learn is by doing. I tell my daughters the same thing, and I'm going to demonstrate the learn-by-doing adage by walking you through the same process I use when I plan to design a new product to sell on Amazon. Maybe you've invented something of your own? Or perhaps you're looking to improve upon a product that is already selling well on the platform. Let's use water bottles as an example. Just about everyone I know has at least one reusable water bottle. The range of these bottles, in terms of color, shape, and size, is also vast, and I can't go anywhere without being reminded to stay hydrated! Water bottles are ubiquitous, which makes them a good model for our new product research.

Nafeeko Case Study, Part 1: Do your research
Enter the words "water bottle" into the Amazon Search Box

What pops up is the Search Results Page (SRP) with about 70 water bottle choices on the first page. Search results can vary based on your location and previous search history, so you may want to use an incognito browser or clear your browsing history for cleaner results. Also, try to avoid spending too much time looking at Sponsored Products. A Sponsored Ad means that the Seller paid for placement on the SRP, which skews the information. Instead, look for Organic Best Sellers, products that are performing well with either a Best Seller or Amazon's Choice tag, not a "Sponsored Ad" tag.

A note about the illustrations that follow: They are snapshots in time from Amazon.com, and I guarantee the information in these images won't be the same by the time this book goes to print. However, the steps you're about to follow remain the same.

Notice that on this first row of products there are three "Sponsored" products and one "Amazon's Choice." The Amazon's Choice product has the #1 Organic Search Results spot for the keyword phrase "water bottles," which means this thing must be a good seller. But how can we be certain?

Click on the Contigo AUTOSEAL Chill Vacuum-Insulated Stainless Steel Water Bottle and follow the link to the Product Details Page (PDP)

Sponsored ⓘ
Cactaki Water Bottle with Time Marker, Large BPA Free Water Bottle, Non-Toxic, 1 Liter 32 Oz, for Fitness and Outdoor Enthusiasts, Leakproof and...
⭐⭐⭐⭐☆ ⌄ 2,723
$19⁹⁹ $24.95
✓prime FREE Delivery Wed, Nov 13

Sponsored ⓘ
Simple Modern Bolt Sports Water Bottle - Insulated Narrow Mouth 18/8 Stainless Steel
⭐⭐⭐⭐☆ ⌄ 585
$15⁹⁹
✓prime FREE Delivery Wed, Nov 13

Sponsored ⓘ
Simple Modern Ascent Water Bottle - Narrow Mouth, Vacuum Insulated, Double Wall, 18/8 Stainless Steel Powder Coated
⭐⭐⭐⭐☆ ⌄ 2,584
$13⁹⁹
FREE Delivery for Prime members

Contigo AUTOSEAL Chill Vacuum-Insulated Stainless Steel Water Bottle, 24 oz., Monaco
⭐⭐⭐⭐☆ ⌄ 3,850
$18⁴² $22.99
✓prime FREE Delivery Wed, Nov 13
More Buying Choices
$15.20 (14 used & new offers)

Scroll to the product detail section on the PDP.

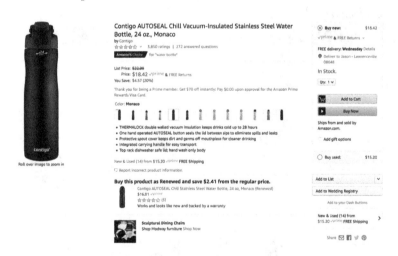

Scroll down to the Product Information Section. Note the product is ranked #8 in the subcategory "Water Bottles." It's also ranked #4 in "Thermoses."

I'm also going to check the Amazon Best Sellers page by clicking on the blue sub-category name, Water Bottles. You can see that at the time of these screenshots, the Contigo Autoseal is indeed ranked #8 in the Water Bottles category.

Spend some time scrolling through this Best Sellers page.

Although your web-based research software may show you that there are better selling products from the search results outside this page, The Amazon Best Sellers Page shows 100 of the best historical sellers on

Amazon over a prolonged period of time, across thousands of water bottles. Products that make it onto this page are the real deal.

As I scroll through these top sellers, I see a lot of great water bottles. There are stainless steel bottles, BPA-free plastic, silicone, insulated and non-insulated bottles. There are bottles for kids and adult bottles. There are some that allow you to filter your water and others that allow you to infuse fruit. I even see replacement parts, like caps and straws for best-selling bottles. So how in the world do I pick a bottle that could compete with this great group of products? Now we're getting into my absolute favorite part of selling on Amazon. We're going to look for the losers. And what I really mean by that is we're going to look for our opportunity to create a winner.

Let's start by looking at the great selling products with a slew of bad reviews, 4 stars or fewer. As I scroll through the Top Sellers, the following water bottles have some problematic issues, along with great sales. Here's what I came up with:

- ✓ The CamelBak Eddy Kids Water Bottle
- ✓ Contigo Autospout Straw Ashland Water Bottle
- ✓ CamelBak Eddy Water Bottle
- ✓ Pogo Plastic Water Bottle
- ✓ Hydro Flask 21 oz. Water Bottle
- ✓ CamelBak Chill Bike Water Bottle
- ✓ Nafeeko Collapsible Water Bottle
- ✓ Nomader Collapsible Water Bottle

This is a pretty substantial list of bottles with potentially fixable issues. The general themes among these eight bottles are "they leak" or "they have an awful taste." Given that this group meets my litmus test for *great sales* and *poor reviews*, I'm going to choose the one that appeals to me the most: the collapsible water bottle. It just seems more convenient than lugging around a heavier, non-collapsible bottle. I also like the sales estimates for the collapsible water bottles. The Nafeeko is doing at least

$30,000 per color variation, per month, while the Nomader is pulling in about $50,000 per color variation, per month. It looks like I'm not the only one who likes the idea of a collapsible bottle!

STEP 5: HIT THE SWEET SPOT

Now imagine if you solved the problems customers are experiencing with collapsible water bottles, and you followed my reliable steps for getting products ranked higher on Amazon. Then you could have a product generating between $300,000 and $600,000 a year in annual sales. Do you recall in Chapter 1 how just 200,000 Sellers are generating more than $100,000 per year in annual sales; and only 50,000 are doing $500,000+? If you can make this collapsible bottle better, and use my method for besting the competition, then you can be among the elite group of Top Sellers on Amazon.

Here's another thing. I've never heard of the brand Nafeeko and my guess is you haven't either; yet here it is doing $300,000 a year in annual sales. It's certainly not as well-known as CamelBak or Hydro Flask, but it is competing with the Top Sellers because the people behind this brand know what they're doing on Amazon. This is the perfect reason *not* to be discouraged. When you use the *The Amazon Jungle Seller's Survival Guide*, you can compete with the big brands. Ready to learn more? In Chapter 4, we'll take a closer look at what's wrong with the Nafeeko collapsible water bottle, and we'll talk about how to source the product and work with a factory on ways to make a better mousetrap or, in this case, a better water bottle. Let's get started.

CHAPTER SUMMARY

- There are more than half a billion products on Amazon.com and millions of Sellers. These numbers are growing every day. By knowing where to look, using your life experience, and reading a few bad reviews, you can identify the next big opportunity that can catapult your product ahead of the competition.

- No matter how big or nasty Amazon gets, there is always opportunity. Learning how to navigate their platform, utilizing the tools that are available, and taking advantage of lessons learned from a battle-tested Seller can take the guesswork out of getting ahead.

- Amazon has a shortcut to identifying and launching their own private label products for their 70+ brands. They even know where many products are made, and they use these data to undermine Third-Party Sellers. But for every new Amazon private label product that launches, dozens of smart Sellers beat them at their own game, every day.

SECTION II:

Let's Get Started!

Chapter 4:

GET IT MADE. MAKE IT COOL.

"YOU DON'T MAKE YOUR MONEY WHEN YOU SELL YOUR
PRODUCT, YOU MAKE IT WHEN YOU BUY YOUR PRODUCT."

TOMMY THE JEWELER

---

n the previous chapter, I showed you how finding a flawed product is sometimes the surest way to land a great one. I walked you through the **5 Essential Steps for Finding a Winning Product** and, applying these steps, we identified a relatively unknown brand with loads of selling potential. Let's recap this critical exploratory process, then move on to something really fun: *making the product better and making it yours.*

The best way to compete effectively on the Amazon.com platform is to create a great product because a not-so-great product will fail; guaranteed. Two decades of selling thousands of products on Amazon helped me refine my strategy for finding winning products. This reliable, repeatable process is how I protected my Top Seller status for so long. In Chapter 3 I talked about why you must start with a product that moves you. Unless you feel passionate about your own product, you can't expect anyone else to be inspired to make the purchase. To satisfy **Step 1**, we agreed, for the sake of example, that water bottles were something to get excited about because of their constant presence in our daily lives. We entered "Water Bottle" into the Amazon Search Box.

Essential **Step 2** says there's got to be a market for our product. In the previous chapter, I shared the example of my folding-leg game table fiasco. Being excited about a new product is important, but without a market for the concept, I had a container full of losers (and losses). In the example of the water bottle, we looked beyond raw enthusiasm, relying instead on data to show us whether the market was hot. After running a search on the words "water bottle," we looked past the sponsored products to the organic best sellers. The Contigo Autoseal bottle rose to the top of our search, complete with the Amazon Choice badge. Our Contigo pick ranked high in more than one category, which signaled we were on the right trail.

In **Step 3** we put our hypothesis to the test, with the help of a web-based research tool that calculates monthly sales quantities for competing products on an Amazon Search Results page. We then viewed the Product Detail Page (PDP) to learn more and discovered Contigo was ranked high in two categories, Water Bottles and Thermoses, which led us to the Amazon Best Sellers Page, where the product was still ranked high (#8) at the time of my original search. This is a hot product!

Step 4 is my favorite part of the research phase. It's where we take the data we've collected to show us the winners; then we sort it for the losers. Great selling products with bad reviews offer the greatest opportunity to get ahead on Amazon. When we selected the Top 100 for bad reviews, we wound up with a small group, from which I picked the one that appealed to me most: The Nafeeko Collapsible Water Bottle.

Over the several pages, we're going to take a closer look at what's wrong with the Nafeeko bottle and how to fix it, source it, and get ready to land it, which will carry us to **Step 5**: Make it better; make it yours.

BAD REVIEW? GOOD OMEN.

Let's talk for a minute about bad reviews. I run into Sellers on a weekly basis who get really fired up about bad product reviews, now called ratings, they receive for their product. I get it. They've invested real money and countless hours bringing the product into the world only to have someone they have never met criticize their baby. It stings. However, if you only take one thing away from this book, know this: *product ratings are gold*. Remember our collapsible water bottle opportunity? The bad reviews from that good-selling product are going to help us develop the next great collapsible water bottle. Furthermore, when you finally land that awesome thing and start selling it, you'll use customer feedback to improve your product further. It's how you discover what you missed in the development and production process from people with a vested interest in your product. Set your ego aside and take in that free gold from your customers. Use it to improve your product every time you reorder, until it's perfect. I feel like listening is a lost art. If you can simply listen, you can increase your sales on Amazon and build a one-of-a-kind, untouchable brand.

WHAT'S YOUR PRICE?

Before I show you how to make your hidden gem cooler using feedback from the bad reviews, let's first be sure we can get it sourced and made for a price that will support the necessary upgrades. I'll start by sharing a story about a friend of mine who once gave me advice I'll never forget. I think I'd been in business for two years when I first met Tommy the Jeweler. Tommy married my Aunt Liz and one evening, while having a Kosher meal in Encino, California, we got into a conversation about business. Tommy had 50 years of experience in the diamond business, and he was asking me lots of questions about this "internet business" my brothers and I had started. I could tell by the quality of his questions that Tommy understood business on a very deep level. He listened intently, then paused before offering this: "You don't make your money when you sell your product, you make it when you buy your product." He then sat back, with a satisfied grin, and he watched me process what he'd just said. I puzzled over it, then countered with my own remark: "I make my money when I sell my product and my customer's credit card gets processed." Tommy punched back. "How much did it cost you?" He asked. "Was there money left after the sale to pay your bills?" Ah, finally. The light bulb turned on. I got it. What Tommy was really saying was that buying a product at the right price was the most important part, especially if you know what people are willing to pay. If I sold my product for $2, for example, because that is what people were willing to pay for similar items, but it cost me $2 to buy it; then I didn't make any money. But if I bought it at the right price, say $0.50, and sold it for $2, then I made money. You don't make your money when you sell your product, you make it when you buy your product. Not only did I finally get it; I never forgot it.

Before we get back to the Nafeeko bottle, let's zero in on the numbers. The minimum cost numbers I'm about to share with you don't necessarily apply across all categories. Some categories are more profitable than others; some have higher return rates. As we factor these variables into our overall assessment, please keep in mind that I'm using rough estimates for where you want to be. Here's an example of how my profitability looked in 2014 before sponsored ads became necessary:

2014 Profitability Table

Retail Price	100%
Cost of Goods Sold (COGS)	-50%
Seller Fee	-15%
Shipping	-15%
Gross Profit	**20%**

*I like to work with cost percentages because they are scalable.

Boy, those were the days! Before the necessity to advertise on Amazon became a thing, you could easily land a product for 50% of the retail price and still make a healthy profit. Not anymore. Now, paying for traffic is a must and the price of poker, as my dad used to say, just went up. Here's what your margin looks like today, with some exceptions, if you pay 50% of your retail price for your goods:

2020 Profitability Table

Retail Price	100%
Cost of Goods Sold (COGS)	-50%
Seller Fee	-15%
Shipping	-15%
Marketing/Advertising	-15%*
Gross Profit	**5%**

*Increasing quarterly

In just a few short years, due to the need to pay for traffic to your listings, margins have taken a 15 point nosedive. I've gone on record in the press about my dislike of Amazon Ads because I feel strongly that products should rank based on their merits. I am also a realist, and I have trained my team (and disciplined myself) to be really good at managing these ads. We manage ads first for search and sales rank and, after optimizing campaigns for a period of time, we then manage the ads for profitability. We'll dive into ads more deeply in Chapter 9.

In today's world, if you can get a product landed for 30% of the retail price, you'll be safer and much happier. That's not always possible on the first few orders, but once your product is improved, ranked, and starts earning good reviews, you'll begin selling a lot more volume. More volume means lower prices from your supplier or factory, too. Plus, once your product rises in the rankings, you'll also gain pricing power. That's right! Once your listings get ranked, you can begin to raise prices and your quantity sold will not decrease. I've done this with hundreds of products and it works every time.

Let's return to our water bottle example and apply what we've just learned about testing for profitability. At the time I pulled the information for this example, The Nefeeko Collapsible Water Bottle was selling for $15.95. If we want to compete with this particular product, then we want to set a landed cost target of 30-40% of retail, or $4.80. The Nomader Collapsible Water Bottle sells for even more at $24.95, so the landed cost target is around $7.50. Can we get these products made for these targeted amounts? Let's find out.

While this book isn't about product sourcing or how to manage your supply chain, I've learned a few things over the years that I think will help point you in the right direction, especially if you've never sourced a product before. Already sourcing? Perhaps the following steps can save you some heartache. I'll confess, most of these lessons came the hard way, and I share them willingly so you may avoid some of the same mistakes I've made.

PRODUCT SPECIFICATION SHEET (PSS)

The Product Specification Sheet (PSS) is the best way to communicate with the factory about what you want to get made. Your first PSS won't be perfect because you're still learning about your product. That said, the product materials and specifications of competing products can teach you a lot about your own. Brands with their own websites often add a ton of product details about their products. As you learn more about what materials work best, your PSS will gradually become more complete.

I've included an example of a very simple PSS that I've used for hundreds of successful products. You can download my spreadsheet for free at Avenue7Media.com, listed on the Resources page at the back of this book. I always find that fiddling around with the real thing makes the process a lot more tangible.

Create a Basic Product Spec Sheet

- Include and image or graphic
- Include as much detail as possible
- Email it to several factories to learn the market price
- Don't forget about packaging!
- Request 2-3 samples for approval

PRODUCT SPECIFICATION & QUOTATION REQUEST FORM

FIND A FACTORY (OR FIVE)

Whether domestic or international, you want to be sure the factory you choose is willing and able to make the product you want, unique to your specifications. Paying a little more, for example, may save you a lot of headaches. Most importantly, you want a factory that is willing and capable of making your product unique to you, incorporating the changes and enhancements you've identified with help from customer feedback and reviews. Remember, *the Amazon advantage comes when Third-Party Sellers improve upon the original product design.*

Before you reach out to a factory with a request for pricing, here are a few things to keep in mind: First, avoid Alibaba like the plague. There are a million YouTube videos that will tell you something different. Don't fall for it. I have never sourced a product on Alibaba and I never will because they don't offer the opportunity to develop a relationship with the manufacturer. Most of the time you'll wind up with a sales rep (or three), which means your cost is going to be much higher than if you work directly with a factory. Additionally, you won't have a direct connection to a factory engineer, which means the unique changes you want to make—the "fixes" that will turn your ugly duckling into a swan—won't be communicated effectively, if at all. The key to your success at this critical juncture is to find a factory (or factories) who'll work with you as a partner. Following are some tips for navigating these important relationships, whether domestic or overseas.

Made in the USA

Once the PSS worksheet is drafted, we're going to begin our factory outreach with a Request for Pricing (RFP), for which a sample is also available on my website. When my brothers and I were first getting started, we focused primarily on American factories. They are generally less expensive to visit; plus, there are still great factories in the good 'ole U.S. of A. In fact, there are a lot of them. An excellent, free resource for finding factories in the United States is Thomasnet.com, a leading product sourcing and supplier discovery platform. There you can search for the product category you want, and you can find any number of domestic factories. You've got to be careful, however, because some of those are importers. Another obvious advantage of sourcing locally is the lack of language barriers. All parties generally speak English and you can therefore better articulate your vision for the product. An American factory will likely also have a better understanding of the domestic market.

Sourcing Overseas

When I was searching for factories overseas, I used software that aggregates U.S. Customs export and import data from countries exporting into the United States. Software like Panjiva, Import Genius, and Data-myne can be expensive, but they're well worth the cost. And they're easy to use. After subscribing, simply search for your product, let's say "water bottles," and you'll get a list of dozens of factories in many countries that are already making them. You'll also get email information, contact information, and reviews on their service and quality. Ideally, you want an overseas factory that makes your product (or similar products) and is exporting to the United States. If they are already exporting products here, then they're used to getting feedback from their U.S. customers about the demands of U.S. end-users.

Here are some other things to consider: Does the factory have a good English speaker on staff? Do they respond promptly to phone or email communications? Can they fix the problems you've identified in the existing product, the one that is similar to yours and is currently on the market? You want a factory that is already familiar with the challenges of making U.S. customers happy. This connection, even if the factory address is half a world away, cuts through a ton of the madness and chaos associated with getting your product sourced. Use one of the export soft-ware services I shared with you above; then spark up a relationship with the factory that feels best. While there are potentially more obstacles in sourcing products overseas, it is always a far better option than using Alibaba.

RUN THE NUMBERS

Now it is time to figure out whether your snappy new product can make you money. You've submitted your Product Specification Sheet (PSS) with Request for Pricing (RFP) information to several factories. Once you hear back about pricing, you'll have an idea of the market cost for getting your product made, as well as information about minimum order quantities and how long it will take to get it made. With this information we can finally run the numbers.

Plug in the cost figures

Add the newly landed cost figures into your PSS, along with your retail price and the Amazon fees, and let's see what happens. Can you net 5%-15% on your first order? If so, you have yourself a winner. It's also important to estimate costs for returns and shipping damage. You won't know for sure until you build up some selling history, but I would recommend factoring in 2% to 5% of sales, depending on your product category. If your category is Apparel or Shoes, your margins will be higher (so will your return rates), so factor in a higher percentage. You may be able to recoup some of those additional costs by reselling your returns as *new* or, on the gray market, as *gently used.*

Build every anticipated cost into your PSS

After everything has been factored in and you've still got a profit—even a single or a low double-digit percentage of profit—then I would recommend you move ahead with your product. Remember, as you sell more volume, your cost of goods will go down. More importantly, as your product climbs in the ranks or even becomes a bestseller with great reviews, you'll be able to raise your retail price and grow your profit further. Factories love volume, and they will reward you with quantity price breaks upon reorder. Amazon loves sales, and they will reward you with better digital real estate and higher visibility, which drive even more sales. We call this phenomenon the Flywheel effect.

MAKE IT COOL. MAKE IT YOURS.

Once you've run the numbers and determined that your product can be profitable (and you've got a factory lined up to build your mousetrap), it's time to apply some creative moxie. This next section is the most subjective part of the product development phase (and the most creative). It's the part where you transform the boring, run-of-the-mill product into the product they can't live without.

Design

Now, straight up, I'm not an industrial designer or a product engineer. I'm not even an artist or a graphic designer. But I do know something about pop culture and where to look for what's trending and cool. When I start designing a new product, I create a Google Folder. I call it my Inspiration Folder, and I stuff it full of popular images from movies and musical artists. I visit popular websites and grab screenshots of things that are trending. Classic designs work well too. For example, Table Tennis was a big category for my Harvil brand, but the designs had become stale. At the time, we were creating some really high-end table tennis tables, but I felt that the tables at the lower price points were really boring. For the redesign, I kept what I call the "bones" of the table the same, focusing instead on new painting schemes that would help differentiate our product from the others on the market. Blue was the most popular color for ping pong tables at the time, so I started a folder with cool-looking blue things. What got me really excited was this 1967 Ford Mustang—white with blue racing stripes. I don't care who you are or where you come from, you have to admit this beauty is cool, right?

Whether you agree with me or not, you might rightly be wondering what the car has to do with table tennis? Fair question. Because I'm not a great artist myself, I let the real designers meld these concepts together. Hiring a graphic designer, unless you've got the chops, will help you with these design challenges. I shared this image with mine, and I asked for three different color schemes that would reflect the sharpness of the Mustang photograph. This was my favorite version, which later got enhanced even further with a dual stripe down the middle (not shown here).

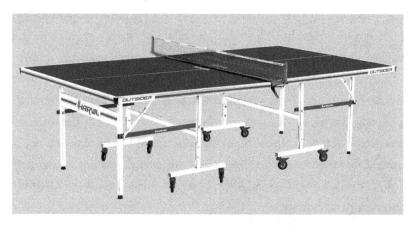

While the table obviously lacks the smooth contours of the '67 GT500, our table popped to the top of the Amazon Search Results Page, and our sales doubled in 60 days. In this second example, the bland purple and white table below was a best-selling competitor on Amazon. My brothers and I thought the design was tired, so I began dropping images of cool snowboard and surfboard designs into a new inspiration folder. What really caught my attention was a cool pair of board shorts I found at the mall, a complex that has since been bulldozed thanks to Amazon competition.

The shorts were orange with cool shades of blue, and I loved how the design intertwined the two colors. I snapped a picture with my phone

and asked my designer to make an air hockey table based on the board shorts' design. Here is how it turned out.

At the time, this design was by far the cleanest and brightest on Amazon, and it quickly became the #1 seller that holiday season. Without these images, you may not even believe that I used a classic car and a pair of board shorts to create distinctive designs and convert them into top-selling products on Amazon. Steve Jobs was paraphrasing Pablo Picasso when he said that good artists borrow, but great artists steal. He was right (again)! Even without artistic training, you can capture what you think is cool and hire a graphic designer to use your inspiration to create your cool product. It's a process that has worked for me for years, and I hope you can use it to put your own style out there.

Packaging should be cool, too!

A quick note about packaging. If you design the coolest, best product in the world and put it into a shoddy box, you'll wind up with bad reviews. The shipment process is brutal, often starting with bumpy transport to a ship that carries your box, along with millions of others, across an ocean. This treatment is followed by three or four more UPS or FedEx excursions on the way to your customer's home. If your product arrives damaged, it simply doesn't matter how cool it was before it got there. Don't shortchange your packaging. I can tell you from experience that nothing is more frustrating than getting a string of bad reviews that tank your sales and sales rank because you didn't bother to pay the extra 75 cents for sturdier packaging materials.

How can you be sure? One of my favorite things to do when I visit a factory is to take one of my completed products, packaged and ready to go, and I hoist it over my head. You know what happens next! It's an inexpensive way to get my point across to the factories that damage is not an option. The surprised expressions from the factory staff is particularly entertaining as I slam my products onto the ground repeatedly.

INSPECT & RESPECT

Now it's time to place an order. Your costs may be a little bit higher than the first price quote you received because you've made sure your item is designed to look cool and the packaging has been fortified to prevent damage. You're still profitable, so it's time to place your first order. Here are a few things to consider once you place the order:

Inspect samples

Whether you end up sourcing your product in the United States or from another country, you must inspect samples of the product *before* it leaves the factory. If you think that a U.S. factory will ship flawless product without your careful inspection, you are wrong. If you think that a Chinese factory has your back, you're wrong again. Remember this phrase: *They will Respect what you Inspect.* Again, this isn't a book on sourcing, but if you wait until your product lands with issues (like my folding leg tables that didn't fold flat), then you are in for a world of hurt. Catch these problems *before* they leave the factory floor and *before* the factory receives their final payment.

Once you sign off, use an inspection company to make sure your product is produced correctly. There are several good inspection companies that can inspect your goods no matter where your factory is located: QIMA, formerly AsiaInspection.com, is one of my favorites and they have quality control inspectors all over the world, including the United States. QIMA and other inspection companies have great online portals where you can create a quality control (QC) checklist for your first order. Your first checklist won't be perfect, but that's okay. Over time, your customers will teach you what to look for. From my experience, there are common checklist items to watch out for: Are there damages, dents, or scratches? Is the product dirty? Is the packaging what you asked for? Also, ask them to check for some of the same issues your competitors had. Looking back at our Nafeeko example, does it hold water? Does it stand up? I've included a sample check list on my website, for which more information is available on the Resources page, as well as contact information for some of the companies I've referenced in this chapter.

Sample size?

A sample size of 2% to 3% for inspection prior to shipment should produce a comprehensive report of the product defects for your order. Addressing these issues up front is a lifesaver (and money-saver). The factory will respect what you inspect. If you find defects in this sample size, don't approve the order for shipment. Wait until the issues are fixed and let the factory know *they* will be paying for the re-inspection because the defective version of your product wasn't what was agreed upon. I still do this, even with factories I trust. It keeps them honest, and it builds a relationship that will pay off for you and the factory as you grow your business over time. They may push back, but at the end of the day, they're invested in your success too. Once you start logging good reviews with a product that stands out from the pack, you'll be reordering more product from the factory. I always work this fact into my early conversations with any factory with whom I'm doing business. We should both be looking for the win-win opportunity.

LAND IT (AND FBA-IT!)

Congratulations! Your goods have passed first inspection, and they're on the cargo ship, heading to the warehouse. Now is a good time to start working on your product listing so you'll be ready for your first shipment. In the next chapter, we'll dive into the details of listing procedures, but first let's get your product safely into the stock room.

I've talked a lot about the benefits of setting yourself apart from Amazon and your competition. Selling *on* Amazon, not *to* Amazon, for example, and building your brand *off* Amazon as well as *on* to protect your messaging and stay in control. Fulfillment by Amazon (FBA) is the big exception. This is where utilizing Amazon's services is a really good idea because the benefits of FBA far outweigh your costs, in my opinion.

The Prime Badge. Need I go further? FBA is akin to the Good Housekeeping seal of approval because when you sign up for FBA, your product earns the hallowed Prime Badge. There are more than 150 million Prime subscribers who search exclusively for products with the Prime Badge. Having one tagged to your listing can give you as much as a 30% boost in sales.

Amazon is your warehouse. For most new Sellers, the costs associated with renting product storage space and managing outbound shipping, picking, and packing costs are prohibitive because they undercut whatever profit you'd built into your model. With FBA, Amazon takes care of all of that, and they disclose their fee after you set up your Amazon Seller Account and enter your product information, including the shipping, weight, dimensions, and packaging. Amazon will give you an estimate of what it's going to cost for FBA to basically be your warehouse.

Reliable deliveries. Amazon is the number one online retailer in America largely because of FBA. Smart Amazon executives, long before Amazon launched FBA in 2006, noticed that Amazon Sellers had very fast growth trajectories early on, but then their sales ultimately plateaued by year three or four. One of the reasons growth slowed was because fulfillment became complicated and expensive after the Seller reached a certain number of orders per day. Add to that the inherent complication of seasonal spikes, especially in November and December. By taking the burden of fulfillment off the backs of Sellers, sales stopped leveling off and continued their upward trajectory. Shoppers simply didn't realize they "needed" Free, 2-Day (now 1-Day!) deliveries. Now they can't live without it, and I would argue that 3P Sellers can't live without the Prime Badge that comes with having their products in Amazon FBA.

Lower cost. Amazon will bill you for storage on a monthly basis, in addition to the FBA fees for picking, packing, and shipping each order which get billed with each order. In my experience, when shipping from my own warehouse, the outbound shipping costs alone, excluding the pick and pack fees, were the *same price* as the all-inclusive FBA shipping fees with Amazon. If you think your inventory will sit in Amazon's fulfillment centers longer than six months, it's best to find a contract warehouse for long-term storage because Amazon's long term storage fees can be painful. I recommend sending just 45-60 days of inventory into FBA warehouses at a time. You'll avoid extra fees and it'll give you control of your supply chain.

We covered a lot of territory in this chapter and we haven't even set up our Amazon selling account yet. Until the fundamentals, covered in the first four chapters of the *The Amazon Jungle Seller's Survival Guide*, are executed, a selling account won't help you. However, now that your product is heading for the warehouse, it's time to get ready to sell. In Chapter 5, I'll show you how to set up your Amazon Seller Account and get Amazon Brand Registered (a key step!). We'll also talk about creating a knock-out listing, with pictures and videos to demonstrate why your product outshines the competition.

CHAPTER SUMMARY

- Find opportunities by following Jason's 5 Essential Steps for Finding a Winning Product using the Nafeeko water bottle example

- Understand the value of bad reviews in identifying flaws that can be fixed and how this is a great opportunity to make the product better and make it yours.

- Before you invest in fixing what's wrong, find out if you can make a profit. New Amazon ad requirements have made it harder for 3P Sellers to succeed. Follow Jason's rule of thumb to determine if there's enough margin for you to pursue your product (or find another one).

- Learn how to create a Product Specification Sheet (PSS) and use it to bridge communication with your factory. Information on where to download free templates for this and other forms are available on the Resources page at the back of this book.

- Find a factory, domestic or international, that you like and that can land your product at a price that can be profitable.

- Inspect your product before it ships and you'll earn the respect of the factory staff, a critical part of building a successful, long-term relationship with your source. Fulfillment by Amazon (FBA) is a great source for 3P Sellers because of its convenience and affordability.

Chapter 5:

LIST IT TO SELL IT!

"MARKETING IS NO LONGER ABOUT THE STUFF THAT
YOU MAKE, BUT ABOUT THE STORIES YOU TELL."

SETH GODIN

Are you ready? With the process outlined in Chapter 4, we learned how to find a great new product to sell. We talked about adding features and benefits that don't currently exist in the marketplace; details we got by reading negative reviews from Amazon customers who were dissatisfied with good selling products. We looked at creative ways to address the problems that needed fixing, and we found inspiration from pop culture to guide us in making it look cool. We also ran the numbers to ensure the new product would be profitable. Pre-shipment inspection tips were also covered to protect our investment and secure the order; and when we ended the chapter, our product had left the factory and was traveling to the warehouse. Now it's time to list this sucker and release it into the wild! But we're not just going to *list it*; we're going to *list it to sell it!*

Over the next several pages, I'll show you where to go to set up your seller account, conduct keyword research, and optimize your listing through A+ content creation. I'll also touch on the constant changes you'll experience on the Amazon.com platform and how the *launch-listen-learn (repeat!)* formula can help you stay ahead of the game. In chapters 7 and 10, Rick Cesari will go into more detail about using direct-to-consumer marketing strategies for building your brand; but in this chapter, you'll learn about the fundamentals for getting set up and positioned to win on Amazon.

AMAZON SELLER REGISTRATION

Once you've figured out what you plan to sell on Amazon, you'll need to go through the Amazon seller registration process, starting with the selection of your Amazon Seller Account.

If you're going to sell more than 40 products per month (and you will!), set up a Professional Account. It requires a small monthly fee, but lower per-order fees, which means you'll come out ahead in the long run. When you're ready to set up your account, go to the source! There are numerous YouTube videos and other how-to resources online, but you want to go directly to Amazon. Don't use YouTube! I've included a slide from the PowerPoint deck I use when coaching clients about getting started on Amazon. I always instruct new Sellers to use the Amazon Services URL highlighted in the slide. I never use screen shots of the step-by-step process on Amazon because it's *constantly* changing. You'll have better luck going directly to the source and following the Amazon Services links for getting starting online.

While the frequency of Amazon procedural changes makes publishing them in a book problematic, my team at Avenue7Media keeps

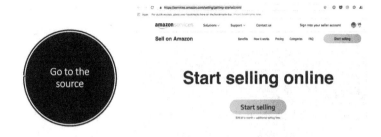

Go to the source

Start selling online

Start selling

basic start-up instructions current on our website. We've set up many new seller accounts, and we create a lot of product listings. As we notice changes on the platform, we update our online documents so that the information is current no matter when you read it. The Resources page at the back of this book will direct you to these instructions. There you go; problem solved!

If you don't have a registered trademark certificate, I highly recommend getting one. You can find an intellectual property (IP) attorney to file your trademark *or* you can use a relatively new service by Amazon called Amazon IP Accelerator. By going through Amazon, you'll get Brand Registry at the moment the attorney files for your trademark rather than waiting until it's officially registered. Brand Registry is a program designed to give brand owners increased control of their products on Amazon.

In my experience, *Brand Registry is a must for Amazon success.* It allows you to create a Brand Store on Amazon, add A+ Content to your product listings, and it provides advertising options beyond what non-brand registered Sellers get. It also gives you control over the content of your product listings. Trust me when I tell you *not* to wait to get a registered trademark! I know people who had trouble getting their trademarks registered and, as a direct result, their listings consistently underperform against competitors who were brand-registered. Already have a registered trademark? Then you're ahead of the game. If not, try Amazon's new IP Accelerator program. I've been impressed with the concept as an easy way to help 3P Sellers get started. If you do try it, my contact information is on the Resources page. Reach out to me on LinkedIn or Twitter; I'd love to hear about your experience!

ARE YOU SEO-FRIENDLY?

In Chapter 3, I talked about how to conduct valuable research to find a product with the potential to make you an Amazon Top Seller. There's another level of research that happens once you're ready to list the product. While positioning your product to look good on your Amazon listing is important, getting people there in the first place is mission critical. If they don't click to view your link, they won't buy your product—no matter how great the messaging and imagery on your listing. Search Engine Optimization (SEO) is key to getting visitors to your listing.

Search Results Page (SRP) & Click-Through-Rate (CTR)

Before we dive into content creation, it is important to understand the key mechanisms by which shoppers will find your listing. If you don't utilize these tools effectively, you won't close the sale, regardless of how good your listing looks. The Search Results Page (SRP) is the gateway to your product. The vast majority of clicks will originate from an Amazon search, so making sure your product "pops" is important. As we start thinking about the layout and design for our listing, we need to be thinking about the marketing strategies that will help our product stand out from the crowd on the SRP. In the section on Listing Optimization & Content Creation, below, I'll share tips for using photos, infographics, and videos in a way that will get you better results on Amazon. An excellent metric to know whether shoppers are seeing (and liking) your product on the SRP is the click-through-rate (CTR). The CTR is available in the campaign manager of Amazon Seller Central, but only if you've run sponsored ads for your product. (We'll talk more about ads and their impact on CTR in Chapter 9.)

Competitor & Keyword Research

At Avenue7Media, my team does exhaustive and continual research of competitors' products and product categories to help clients better position themselves for success on Amazon. We like to start with competitor and keyword research for two reasons: sales messaging and Search Engine Optimization (SEO). Using best practices for SEO will help your listing rise to Page 1 of the Amazon SRP; and keyword research is the starting point. Yes, we've already done a lot of research to find a winning product, but competitor and keyword research will help ensure that shoppers can find us. When conducting competitor research, we typically start by creating a table with key information about our top competitors, including ASIN (Amazon Standard Identification Number), price, and other helpful data points. I like to use a software tool called Keepa for the range of prices a competitor has been priced over time. With Keepa's Chrome browser extension, the pricing information will load onto each PDP you view. In addition, we add fields to rate the quality of their images, infographics and, because we want to know what's wrong with our competitors' products, we read their 1 and 2-star reviews. Your competitors' bad product reviews will not only help you find a great product to make and improve upon, as we learned in Chapter 4, *but they can also help you sell your new product.*

Let's use our collapsible water bottle as an example. We learned that almost all of the collapsible water bottles on the market leaked, so with the help from our factory engineers we made certain that *our* collapsible water bottle does *not* leak. We also tested these bottles at the factory before they shipped, and we are confident they won't leak. This "competitive intelligence" is what we'll use for our product listings in the bullet points and in the infographics. We may create a bullet point, for example, with an all-caps header that reads, *Guaranteed Not to Leak* or *Leak-proof Technology.* Do you see what we did here? We took the opportunity to explain to an Amazon customer, who may be clicking through several collapsible bottles, that *ours* is better. Keep in mind this method only works if you are 100% confident that your bottles won't leak. That's another reason why, in Chapter 3, we identified all of the competitor defects, we fixed them in our production, and now we're calling out why ours is better. It's a great way to steal away market share from the established players, and it all starts with research.

Keyword research is also critical for identifying words that will direct shoppers to your listing. There are many tools available for identifying keywords to include in your product title, product bullet points, and product description. Let's start with the freebie. We used this method in Chapter 3, when we first started our product research. By simply typing the name of the product into the Amazon search field, you will observe a long list of products called up in response to your query.

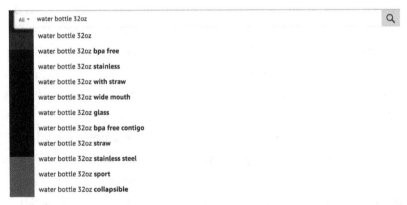

It's not a perfect method, but it's free, and you can let your imagination run wild with different variations of product uses and types to enter into the search prompt. Don't forget to look at other high-volume keywords related to your product. The free AMZ Suggestion Expander is another favorite tool of mine. It multiplies the number of keyword suggestions right on the Amazon search page. The Avenue7 team also runs reports to identify longer tail keywords or keywords further down the purchase funnel. For our water bottle example, "water bottle" is a top-of-the-funnel keyword, compared to longer tail words like blue water bottles, silicone water bottles or, you guessed it, collapsible water bottles. Because our product is in fact a collapsible water bottle, we want to make sure this keyword phrase, and at least two others, are represented well in our product title and in our bullet points. But wait. If Amazon's search algorithm looks for keywords, why can't I just repeat the top keywords, 1,000 or more times, in the copy of my listing? I wish. But trust me; it won't work. Just like Google's search algorithm, Amazon's algorithm gets smarter by the day, and it rewards well-written copy with a reasonable representation of keywords. At the writing of this book, I am finding that it works best to duplicate your top keywords at least twice in just two of the following sections: (1) In the product title, the bullet points, and the product description; as well as (2) in the backend keywords section of the Seller Central account. Algorithms change and strategies like this one have to be adjusted, but there are some great resources and blogs out there that can help you stay on top of the search optimization game. One of my favorite blogs is Sellics.com. I like it especially when it comes to Organic Search Rank.

LISTING OPTIMIZATION & CONTENT CREATION

Better understanding about how keywords work and of the value of standing out on the search results page will help guide you in the creation of a compelling listing. I always tell my clients that anyone can create an Amazon listing, but it takes an expert to create a listing that sells. Over the next several pages, I will share the same strategies I've used repeatedly as a Seller and as a consultant to help clients optimize their listings and boost their sales on the Amazon.com platform. Before we get creative, let's take a tour of the virtual layout Amazon provides for showcasing your product. The good news is for 3P Sellers: now there is a lot more real estate to play with than there was back when I started!

"Above the Fold"

Back in the golden age of printed newspapers, advertisers competed for favorable placements that were high on the page or "above the fold." In digital marketing and advertising, the fold varies depending on the resolution settings on a visitor's monitor, but the concept is the same. It the part of your screen available without having to scroll down the page. Just like the day's biggest headlines, you want the most important messaging about your product to feature prominently on your Amazon Product Detail Page. In my experience, this section is the foundation of success on Amazon. If the "above the fold" imagery and messaging is bad, nothing else will work, including ads.

Here's an example of a listing my agency created for a client. My team of graphic designers and video editors used clear, professional product shots, plus infographics and a video demonstration (one of the seven thumbnail images on the left) to deliver the product-benefits message. With Brand Registry, you'll have the opportunity to go into even greater depth about your product, which we'll talk more about next. But making a strong first impression here, at the top of the page, is key to making the sale.

Amazon A+ Content

Formerly called Enhanced Brand Content, Amazon A+ Content is the tool that enables brand owners to describe product features in an advanced way, e.g. add detailed descriptions, charts, high-quality images, and custom copy (brand stories). The A+ section gives shoppers more information about the product, but more importantly, they give you the chance to build a relationship with prospective customers and strengthen your brand. When done right, A+ Content can give you a double-digit lift in sales conversions. It's like your own product endorsement page, and a space where you can connect with prospective customers. Here's a page my team created for the Jewelry Spa Hot Tub Jewelry Cleaning System.

YOUR JEWELRY NEVER FELT SO CLEAN!
Enjoy the compliments when your jewelry sparkles like new. Safely bring dull, lifeless jewelry back to life with the one-of-a-kind Jewelry Spa HOT TUB!

WHY IT WORKS SO WELL
Effectively cleans in 3 ways:

1. Through **Thermal Heat Energy** when the solution is microwave-heated to its ideal cleaning temperature

2. Through the **Naturally-Based Condensed Green Solution** that gently eliminates germs, bacteria, hand soap residue, and offensive odor

3. Through **Spin Swish Mechanical Energy** that makes your jewelry sparkle like brand new

THE BENEFITS OF USING THE JEWELRY SPA HOT TUB

FAST, EASY, AND AFFORDABLE
The Jewelry Spa Hot Tub is light, easy-to-use, and fast! It cleans your jewelry in as little as 5 minutes! (Cleaning times may vary). It will not damage your jewelry either when used as directed. Each 6-oz bottle of the green cleaning solution makes 2 reusable 12-oz baths and each bath cleans 50 to 75 pieces of jewelry. That's up to 150 cleanings in one bottle!

THE ONLY JEWELRY CLEANER TO REMOVE TARNISH AND DANGEROUS BACTERIA
The Jewelry Spa Hot Tub Cleaning Kit can remove jewelry tarnish unlike other jewelry cleaners including ultrasonic jewelry cleaner. Our highly effective jewelry cleaning solution thermally eliminates jewelry germs caused by sebum, sweat, bacteria, makeup, soap, and grime so that your jewelry looks like new.

REMOVES EMBARRASSING JEWELRY ODORS
Our jewelry cleaning kit uses a jewelry cleaner liquid solution formulated with green ingredients such as purified water, organic alcohol, and plant extracts to gently disinfect and sanitize your jewelry; removing embarrassing jewelry odors so that it smells like new.

LEAVES YOUR SKIN FREE FROM BLACK MARKS AND RASHES
With the Jewelry Spa Hot Tub, you can now enjoy wearing your jewelry without the worry of having black marks and rashes on your finger, neck or skin.

Amazon provides several templates from which to choose. I recommend combining some basic brand identity and brand messaging, along with much more detail about the additional product benefits to the customer. I'm always amazed by how much conversion rates improve when we add A+ Content to a listing, especially considering how far down customers have to scroll to find it!

Design your own store

Once your A+ Content is completed you'll have the opportunity to build your own Amazon Brand Store, another feature available only to Sellers who are Brand Registered. I like to think of it as my own website on Amazon. Your Amazon store is the ideal landing page for driving off-Amazon traffic to your listings. You can create source tags, too, for links to your Amazon store from Facebook or Instagram, which allows you to test what traffic channels work best. Amazon loves off-Amazon-to-Amazon traffic, something Rick will talk about in depth in Chapter 10. For now, know that sending traffic to your Amazon Brand Store can help boost your Amazon sales and grow your brand.

The Amazon Brand Store allows you to add multiple pages as tabs, share your origin story, and upload videos—a far cry from the old days of Amazon, when Sellers only had space for a few extra images, no A+ details, and certainly no store! For the Jewelry Spa Hot Tub, we really needed that extra space because of the product's long list of benefits. It can literally clean every type of jewelry and, with the Amazon Brand Store, we had the space to deliver all of those details in a compelling way. There is a lot about Amazon that can be frustrating, but they've done a good job offering up the space to show your brand in the best possible light—a win-win for Amazon *and* for Sellers.

DO YOU KNOW WHO YOUR CUSTOMER IS?

We're making progress now. You have a Seller's account, your product

YOUR JEWELRY NEVER FELT SO CLEAN!

Enjoy the compliments when your jewelry sparkles like new.

Safely bring dull, lifeless, jewelry back to life with the one-of-a-kind **Jewelry Spa HOT TUB!**

No more black marks or rashes on your finger, neck or skin.

Removes embarrassing jewelry odors so that it smells like new

is brand registered, and you're going to take full advantage of the various content pages available to 3P Sellers. But before you start populating these spaces with information about your product, are you sure you know—I mean *really* know—who your target audience is? Maybe this seems like an obvious question, but you'd be surprised how many Sellers I've met who don't fully understand to whom they are marketing. If that's the case, then you'll waste a heck of a lot of time developing your message and building up content for the wrong audience.

How do you find out what your customer profiles or demographics actually look like? In my professional experience, I've found that using a mailing list broker, like ManageByStats or Infogroup, helps immensely in sifting through the data. These data companies can quickly and accurately return information about customers' ages, geographic areas, household income, home type, whether or not they have children, and a whole lot more. These avatars or customer profiles are invaluable when you are deciding how to approach the content-development phase of creating (and optimizing) your listing. What kind of model should I use in the photos (and videos) I select? How should my copy read? Am I talking to an older audience or a younger group? Does my product appeal to active women or men (or both?!). The information you glean from these data companies will guide you in crafting a strong, effective, targeted message.

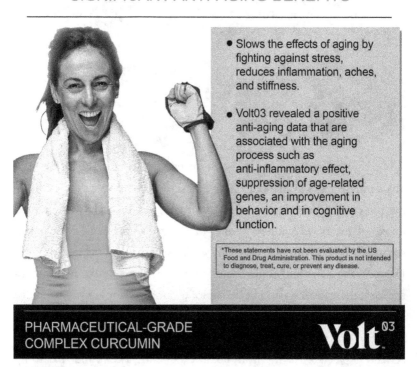

FIRST SUPPLEMENT TO DEMONSTRATE SIGNIFICANT ANTI-AGING BENEFITS

- Slows the effects of aging by fighting against stress, reduces inflammation, aches, and stiffness.

- Volt03 revealed a positive anti-aging data that are associated with the aging process such as anti-inflammatory effect, suppression of age-related genes, an improvement in behavior and in cognitive function.

*These statements have not been evaluated by the US Food and Drug Administration. This product is not intended to diagnose, treat, cure, or prevent any disease.

PHARMACEUTICAL-GRADE
COMPLEX CURCUMIN

Volt 03

Once you've identified your customer, it's a heck of a lot easier to determine the types of lifestyle images, for example, that you want for your products. I love this image of a fit, active woman raising her fist in this infographic we used for a client who is selling a supplement known for its anti-aging benefits. The idea here is that our target audience will identify with this person—want to be and feel like this person—and be compelled to learn more about the product as a result. (Notice we've also layered branding on the footer.)

Features tell, benefits sell

I know I've brought this up before, and you'll hear more about it from Rick in Chapter 7; but I can't stress this enough: *features tell, benefits sell*. It frustrates me to see how many Amazon product listings still focus on the features of the product rather than the benefits. Let's apply this *benefits sell* theory to the water bottle that our factory helped us modify in Chapter 4. One of the features that make it collapsible is the non-toxic silicone material. This is an important feature, and something that didn't need fixing from the original source. But the features are *not* the most important part of our messaging. But what if we looked at it in a different way? The silicone we used is food-grade quality and won't cause harm when you drink from it. The fact that *our product is safe,* too, is an enormous benefit and something I know I look for when buying products that my family consumes. It's also collapsible, which is another great feature, but what about it? I believe it's the fact that you can easily store it after it's empty that's appealing to people who are stuck lugging heavy, hard-to-stow bottles around at the end of a long hike. If you are tempted to carry plastic water bottles because they're lighter, now you don't have to, which is better for the environment. These are the details we want to emphasize in our messaging. We want to answer the shopper's question, *what's in it for me,* before he or she even has to ask.

Remember my game tables? I've talked about my epic foosball fail, where I ran with my Big Idea before doing the necessary market research. Ouch! But here's a different kind of story, one where following my own advice paid off, handsomely. The air hockey tables my brothers and I designed were loaded with dozens of great features, like strong blower motors for consistent airflow, collapsible steel rods, and environmentally-friendly wood. These tables were top quality, and having played a role in ensuring the quality of the components, I can tell you it was hard not to lead with these sweet details. Instead, we focused on the *key benefits* of our tables, like bringing friends and families together. You don't buy a foosball table because of its features. You buy it because you want to have more fun with your friends and loved ones. While our competitors were writing about the thickness of the wood and the types of steel rods *they* were using in their products, *we* were focused on the end result—fun. And safety! We paid extra for telescoping rods because they are safer for kids, and parents truly appreciated those facts.

It also helped that our tables were positively reviewed and made from quality materials. There's a place for highlighting these kinds of details in your listing. But because every word (and image!) counts, you want to maximize the benefits of your own messaging by *developing content with the end-result in mind*. With the right message, good copy, sharp images (and video!) you can leap frog past your competition. Let's spend a minute on each of these fundamentals.

Copy matters!

Whether writing copy for your listing or a script for video, it's the copy that can persuade people to stick with you long enough to hear the offer. When Rick talks to you about marketing in the Chapter 7, you'll appreciate that he got his start 40 years ago selling suntan lotion on the beach in Florida. When he talks about the lessons learned from his "towel-to-towel" strategy, he says he learned that the customer is the absolute best source for content. Rick always starts a new project by interviewing 15-20 people who've used the product and are willing to provide a testimonial about their experience. He reminds me to listen for "kernels of truth" about what they like and don't like. The answers to the best marketing campaigns are always there!

Read the Reviews

If there are 500 reviews about your product, read all 500. A theme will emerge that can help you craft a more effective message. This feedback loop is not only a great source of information for learning what's wrong with your product and fixing the problem, but it can tell you what's *right* about your product so you can call it out in your messaging.

Cut to the chase with infographics

We all know that it's more fun to look at pretty pictures or watch cool videos than it is to read plain text. Let's face it. While content is important, people don't read as much as they used to, which means your messaging has to fit into your headers. To the extent you can tie these headers to an image, then you're in a much better position to get your message *heard*. An infographic is a convenient hybrid of text and image, and when they are used properly, infographics can really help call out information that might otherwise be overlooked. They are a great tool for marketing because most people tend to remember what they saw more than what they read. Infographics are also a great way to utilizing the finite space we have on the PDP, above the fold. For the Jewelry Spa Hot Tub, we used a close-up from one of our infographics to call out one of the product's key benefits: *The only jewelry cleaner to remove tarnish and dangerous bacteria.*

Finding innovative ways to showcase a product's benefits, in easily digestible pictures, will help ensure your customers are hooked from the start.

THE ONLY JEWELRY CLEANER TO REMOVE
TARNISH AND DANGEROUS BACTERIA

ELIMINATES JEWELRY GERMS CAUSED BY
SEBUM, SWEAT, BACTERIA, MAKEUP, SOAP, AND GRIME
SO THAT YOUR JEWELRY LOOKS LIKE NEW!

Jewelry Spa®
HOT TUB

A picture truly is worth 1,000 words

Before you rush the photography process and upload unprofessional images that don't adequately represent your product, you may be interested to know that product photography directly affects clicks and conversions. Amazon has a full list of requirements when it comes to images, but they are most restrictive about the first image, or the Main Image. The main image should be high resolution and on a white background only. I ask my clients for very large images, as large as 2500 pixels and 300 dpi. If that doesn't mean anything to you, it will to your graphic designer. Image work is where a good graphic designer can be worth their weight in gold. Avoid short cuts at this stage, if at all possible. Your first product image must be sharp, bright, and stand out on the SRP.

That said, it is the additional images where we close the sale. I recommend outlining every additional image with your brand color scheme and logo, using lifestyle images where ever possible. I look for people who look like our customer and who are happy, aspirational types, interacting with the product. Here's an example we used for the Harvil ping pong table:

These shoots can be expensive. The photoshoot pictured here cost us $20,000, but we also shot video and 3 other products at the same shoot. The quality of stock photos on sites like Shutterstock and Unsplash are getting better every year. Some of the images are even free! While it will be difficult to find a model interacting with a product just like yours, you can find an image that captures the look and feel of your message and use it in an infographic, where the key information about your product is then visually connected to the image. Here are some other tips to consider:

Make a good first impression. People form a first impression in a fraction of a second. On Amazon, the "hero image" is the first thing a shopper sees when browsing. Most shoppers are not choosing which items to click on by reading the title, but are instead making quick decisions based on the images they see.

Engage customers. A high-quality image will grab the attention of shoppers and make them more likely to stick around. Photos draw the customer in and encourage them to learn more about your product, which when paired with engaging product information, can nudge them to purchase.

Increase the perceived quality of your product. Badly lit or unprofessional photos can quickly make your product seem cheap and undesirable. Even if you are selling a high-end product, a grainy product image will bring down the perceived value of your brand and customers will likely not bother to learn more.

Reinforce your brand message. Photos should always tie in with your overall branding goal. Generic or photo-shopped images tell shoppers nothing about your brand or product. Presenting a cohesive brand across all marketing fronts will reinforce a professional image and make shoppers more confident in purchasing from you.

Video persuasion

Rick has used video persuasion techniques to create television and online ads that have driven millions of dollars in sales and established numerous brands—brands you may well use in your home today, leading to more than $4 billion in direct-to-consumer sales. He loves to remind me that while the technology has certainly changed over the past three decades, what motivates people hasn't, and video remains the most effective way to appeal to people. It is also key to building your brand. I've watched over the years as Amazon has become a product demonstration video platform. I won't list a product anymore without it. Rick will talk later about what types of videos work best. For now, here are some pretty amazing stats that drive home the value of using video on Amazon:

Every second nearly 17,000 hours of new video will be produced. Forbes reports more videos produced in the last 30 days than television networks have produced in the last 30 years.[13]

Research shows that nearly 80 percent of all internet traffic will be comprised of videos.[14]

Including video on a landing page can increase conversion rates by 80%[15]

The sales and conversion power of video is pretty clear. If you aren't using video in your Amazon listing and on your Brand Page, you should start.

If you are not getting the response you hoped for, don't be afraid to try something different. Change the introduction or cut out a bit that falls flat. In his book, *Video Persuasion*, Rick shares a great example from the very first infomercial he produced for the George Foreman Grill. He thought it would be a good idea to start with boxing footage of George knocking out Michael Moorer to win the heavyweight crown at age 46—the oldest ever. He tested the show, and it didn't work—not even close. He made the common mistake of misreading the target audience, which at the time was primarily stay-at-home moms. Once he removed the boxing footage and changed the introduction to reflect the benefits of the prod-

13 Mary Lister. "37 Staggering Video Marketing Statistics for 2018," The Wordstream Blog. https://www.wordstream.com/blog/ws/2017/03/08/video-marketing-statistics. March 8, 2017.

14 Greg Jarboe. "By 2021, 80% f the World's Internet Traffic Will Be Video," Tubular Insights, November 14, 2017. https://tubularinsights.com/video-2021.

15 Garrett Hughes. "15 high-Converting Landing Pages (That'll Make You Wish You Built 'Em). Unbounce, August, 6, 2019. https://unbounce.com/landing-page-examples/high-converting-landing-pages/

uct, the show took off and became one of the most successful infomercials ever produced. Like Rick, I am constantly fine-tuning my approach to every video I produce. I am fascinated by the surprising ways in which the elements of good video-making can come together to form a winning message. I don't always get it right, but I'm continually learning and open to new and better ways to make meaningful, lasting connections.

LAUNCH. LISTEN. LEARN. (REPEAT!)

Remember when I mentioned that being in the Marines was easier than being an Amazon Seller? Of course that was tongue-in-cheek, but the metaphor about discipline and endless work are true to my experience. The work never stops. Once your product is listed and selling, and you start receiving customer feedback, then you must constantly revisit your listings for areas of improvement. The relationship with your factory is more important than ever as you lean on them to make necessary adjustments. If one customer has a concern or complaint, then more customers likely have (or will have) that same complaint. You can improve your sales if you answer customers' questions *before* they have to ask. It's not unusual for our team to update our clients' listings as many as four times a year. Nothing on Amazon is "set it and forget it," and that goes double for the listings. The Jewelry Spa Hot Tub listings I shared in this chapter have been edited half a dozen times. By the time you read this book, they will likely have been edited half a dozen more. *Vigilance is required to thrive on Amazon.* And while the competition is fierce (and getting fiercer), you can achieve Top Seller status by using the strategies we've talked about and applying them with equal ferocity. In the immortal words of Rocky Balboa, "Every champion was once a contender who refused to give up."

CHANGE. EXPECT IT.

Amazon changes a lot. In 20 years of business, I have never experienced the kind of head-spinning modifications and pivots to a software platform or a company's policies and procedures as often and as rapidly as on Amazon. The website where customers go to make purchases is always evolving, affecting formats, systems, and product placements. Same holds true for the user interface used to create your Seller Central account and product listings. Earlier in the chapter, I told you that Rick and I have created a Resources page at the back of this book, with instructions on where to find samples, references, and a list of our favorite software tools and other resources to help make your transition to Amazon a little bit easier. Over the years, he and I have both benefited from the guidance and support of our mentors and peers. Visual aids and real people to talk to can make a big difference. It's part of what makes this a true *Seller's Survival Guide!* We hope these materials will help you, too.

CHAPTER SUMMARY

- We explored the advantages of setting up a Professional Seller Account; plus, information on utilizing the Amazon IP Accelerator to help businesses more quickly obtain intellectual property (IP) rights and brand protection in Amazon stores.

- Brand Registry is a must for Amazon success because it allows Sellers to create a Brand Store on Amazon, add A+ Content to product listings, and it provides advertising options beyond what's available to non-brand registered Sellers.

- Finding the right keywords for your product is an essential element of becoming an Amazon Top Seller. If shoppers don't click to view your link, they won't buy your product, no matter how great the messaging and imagery on your listing.

- Anyone can create an Amazon listing, but it takes experience to create a listing that sells. Jason offers his tested strategies for optimizing listings and boosting sales on Amazon.

- Start "above the fold" and make it count.

- Amazon has expanded the number of places and spaces for which 3P Sellers can add content. Learning how to access that digital real estate and effectively use the tools for creating strong content can make or break your listing.

- Know who your customer is and design your campaign around your target audience. Focus on the benefits of your product; not just the features.

- Persuasive writing and the use of sharp, professional images and video can enhance your messaging and increase your sales conversion rate.

Chapter 6:

FORGET WHAT YOU KNOW ABOUT RETAIL

"THE MORE I LEARN, THE LESS I REALIZE I KNOW."

SOCRATES

I n our capacity as agency founders and consultants, Rick and I have had the great pleasure of speaking to many companies and brands owners. Many of those brands are well-established with a lot of success selling to buyers at big box retail stores or on television. It's not easy these days to get a product placed in a large retail chain store, and I applaud all of you who are making it work and making a profit. Unfortunately, strategies that work for brands in brick and mortar stores don't translate well on Amazon. Just ask Birkenstock and Nike for proof.

In 2016, Birkenstock's CEO famously said that he would stop selling to Amazon because it was impossible to stop unauthorized Sellers and maintain a clean selling channel on the platform. In 2019, Nike pulled a page from Birkenstock's book and took their brand off Amazon. They were (understandably) pissed that Amazon wasn't playing fair, and they essentially picked up their toys and went home. But that's just it. You can't pick up *all* of your toys because they're *everywhere*. Plus, what's to stop a Third-Party Seller from redirecting the stuff that's out there, back to Amazon? And when they do, you'll no longer be there to control the messaging about your own products. Things can go downhill quickly when you leave behind a void on a platform like Amazon. Someone is going to fill it, and the problem you are running from will rapidly accelerate from bad to worse. One of Mr. Bezos's early strategies for driving prices down was to make it easy for Sellers to attach to someone else's product listing. The premise being that if more Sellers are selling the same product, prices will go down. Boy did they! You may recall Bezos' infamous quote, *Your margin is my opportunity*. It is this ability of Sellers to attach to another product listing, coupled with Amazon's disinterest in stopping unauthorized Sellers from doing so, that drives brands crazy.

What brands have to understand is that Amazon doesn't need them, not even Nike or Birkenstock, because Amazon has an entire army of other Sellers waiting to snatch up diverted products and list them on the Amazon.com marketplace. James Thomson and Whitney Gibson talk in depth about ways in which brands can protect themselves on Amazon, and I strongly recommend their book, *Controlling Your Brand in the Age of Amazon*. These authors pioneered the tactics that protect brands on Amazon, and I guarantee you Nike and Birkenstock would be much happier today if they'd called my good friend James before making such a big mistake. Don't sell *to* Amazon, sell *on* Amazon. Having a Third-Party Seller Central account, along with Brand Registry (and an effective legal strategy), would have helped Nike and Birkenstock clean up their Amazon channels, without waiting for Amazon to do it for them. Amazon isn't going to work for brands in that way. Frankly, you don't want to relinquish that kind of control, which is why I asked you to forget everything you know about retail business. Success with other sales channels, like TV and brick and mortar, does not guarantee success on the Amazon Marketplace. Hard work and an effective brand message that *you* control will pave the way to increased sales and greater awareness of your brand products.

THE AMAZON MINDSET

Over the years I've sold products to large retail chains and sporting goods stores, some of which are now out of business. We always went into these stores at the high-end of the price range. We started our wholesale price high because the retail buyer always required concessions before placing the order, like return allowances or defect allowances, for example. If the product hit the shelves and wasn't selling right away, Walmart would ask its vendors to pay for a mark down; or request money to finance "roll back" pricing deals for their customers. If you refused to pay, they'd not so gently inform you that you would not be invited back to sell there again. So everyone who has ever sold to Walmart, or other big box retailers for that matter, knows that you have to start high. If you don't, you'll lose a lot of money.

I give you this background because what I'm about to say next causes clients to look at me like I've got a foreign object sticking out of my forehead. If you begin your listing priced high on Amazon, you will hear crickets. Let me rephrase that: *If you start high, your product will not sell.* I get approached by brands regularly who tell me Amazon isn't an effective channel for them. It just doesn't work, they say. And that's when I do a little research of my own, and I share how much business their direct competitors are doing each month in the form of sales on Amazon. This is when they usually realize that it's not Amazon that's ineffective; rather, it's their Amazon strategy that is tanking. Most Top Sellers doing hundreds of thousands, even millions a month in sales know one thing: *Amazon listings are an investment.* With Amazon, Search Results are your new buyer, and doing things aggressively to get your products to rank high is critical to your sales success on the platform. Doing them the right way, through your own brand-registered Seller Central account, is imperative and it will turn your hard work into strong rankings. Once your products are scoring high reviews and steadily climbing in the rankings; then (and only then) can you raise your prices.

START LOW, END HIGH.

With Amazon, you are no longer selling to a human buyer. Instead you must feed the algorithm. When Top Sellers launch a new product, they do two things. First, they lower their price (or reduce their price through coupons or special deals) to a break-even point *or lower*. Wait, what? You want me to lose money on a sale at launch? I wish the answer wasn't, yes, but it is, and that's not even the worst part. I also want you to spend as much as 100% of your sales amount on Sponsored Ads in the first 30 days, post-launch. We'll get into the nitty-gritty of Amazon Ads logic in Chapter 9, but follow my rationale here because it's important. In the Amazon jungle, you have to look at each and every product listing as an investment on which you will temporarily lose money on each sale. Additionally, you'll be paying twice your selling price in ads to drive traffic to your listing. The good news? As with any good investment, there is always a payoff.

What you get back for all your cash investment in your product listing is Search Results Page Rank (SRP) and Best Seller Rank (BSR). I actually like to go a step further and rank for Sub-Category Rank (SCR) as well. The more products you sell, the more likely you are to receive Amazon product reviews and ratings, and if your product is good (*Product is King!*) and the reviews are favorable, then Amazon customers will trust your product and buy more.

The more sales you generate with your new product, the more the Amazon ranking algorithm is going to reward your listing with better digital real estate. With this strategy, I've seen products go from *nowhere* to the second page of Search Results in just a few weeks. I've also seen first page SRP results and Top 100 sales rank within 30-90 days. The real growth starts when you break into the Top 20 or Top 10 in sales rank and your product reaches Page 1 for several high-volume, relevant keywords. When your product "indexes" or "ranks," as we call it, your sales will grow exponentially. As your sales and rank grow, along with the volume of good product reviews, you gain pricing power. That's right, now you can begin a gradual price increase back to profitability and beyond, *without* a decrease in sales volume. Raise your price gradually, though, or Amazon will punish your listing with a Buy Box Suppression. When Amazon suppresses your Buy Box, you can no longer drive traffic to your listing and rank can drop fast, so gradually increase your prices by 2%-3% every 2-3 days to avoid it.

Now you can see how this strategy is almost the exact opposite of selling to the big box retail stores. Rather than list your product high, only to have your profit margins whittled away by discounts and fees, you list low, generating more sales and boosting your rank. Only then, on Amazon, are you in a strong position to raise your price, gradually. I can't emphasize this point enough: start low and temporarily exchange profits for sales and search rank. When your product breaks into the Top 10 for your Amazon sub-category, slowly begin to raise your retail price and watch your profits grow. You must remain vigilant and pay close attention to your product and your competition; and you must be willing to offer additional short-term price reductions if rank starts to stall. *Dog-ear this page and come back to it regularly.* The process goes against the grain of more traditional retail practice, but it was key to building my own brand of Top Sellers on Amazon.

Another parallel process worth highlighting is the continual optimization of your Sponsored Ads, which we'll go into later. With Sponsored Ads, or pay-per-click advertising, you pay a specified amount for each click to your listing, casting a very wide net of keywords at the start. Some of these keywords will convert to sales and you'll keep them; others won't (and you'll pause or negate them). This is another key part of the process that can feel counterintuitive, but it is a short-term strategy that will allow you to find the best, most relevant keywords that convert. I'm oversimplifying the optimization process for Sponsored Ads, but know that the low prices/big ad spends don't continue forever; they are merely tools to launch us out of Siberia to the busiest corners of Main Street, USA.

Here's a great visual from our friends at Teikametrics about the typical product campaign life cycle. I've studied this process on thousands of products, and the launch path for all of them looked eerily similar to what's pictured here in this graph. Once a great product starts to gain rank, and the sales line crosses the ad spend line (green over red), you can finally put it on the balance sheet because *now* you have an asset and a winner.

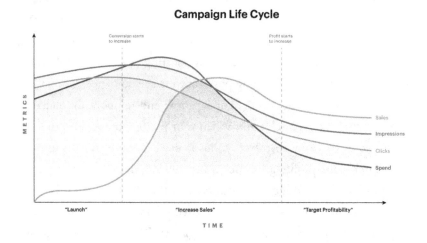

Campaign Life Cycle

SALES RANK METRICS

Now that you understand the proper mindset for Amazon success, it's time for a deep dive into the many metrics we use to measure success and to make corrections if the metrics aren't heading in the right direction.

Product Reviews Are King

In Chapters 3 and 4 I talked a lot about the importance of finding a great product, one you are passionate about, with flaws you can fix, for which there is an eager market. For a not-so-great product without a sizable market, none of these metrics matter. When you source correctly, solve problems in the marketplace, and make your product look cool and distinctive, customers will love it *and sales will grow.*

Product reviews are the absolute best metric to use for how well your product is performing. If your reviews, or ratings (especially with a new launch) remain above four stars, then the future is bright for your product *and* your listing. Studying these reviews, and learning from the bad ones, will help you improve your product each time you reorder from your supplier. Amazon's Customer Q&A feature on the product page is another great place to search for questions your customers have about your product. This information is invaluable to Sellers because these issues can typically be solved. Related issues, like complaints about packaging or delivery can also be resolved, and if you can take this feedback and apply it, then you can resolve these problems so that the next iteration of your product won't draw the same criticism. Stay alert and look for problems. Once fixed, I can guarantee you that your product will have won the battle.

In the previous chapter, we focused on optimizing our listings, with direct response benefits messaging and aspirational images showcasing real people interacting with our product. Even though Amazon restrictions limit what we can do with the Main Images on the PDP, they play a critical role, as do the product titles. If your product has a low click-through-rate (CTR) of 0.10%, then it's time to try new images and/or fix the product-title wording. Amazon only displays CTRs from the Campaign Manager in Seller Central, and you'll only see them from Sponsored Ads campaigns. At the writing of this book, they still won't share CTR for organic listings, but you should be able to get those results by measuring the CTR in Sponsored Ads. The click-through-rate is often overlooked by Sellers, and it shouldn't be. I'm always amazed at how even minor changes to the Main Image and product titles can improve CTR and sales. Because these two features are the most visible from the SRP, make sure they are bright, clear, and get to the point of offer. In doing so, customers looking for products like yours will be more likely to find your listing. I get particularly excited when I see CTRs above 1%. That's confirmation that the Main Image and titles are working for me. This is when all your hard work in creating compelling products and product listing pages pays off. With on-point infographics, aspirational images, a focus on benefits, A+ content, and a strong brand page, shoppers now have every reason they need to buy *your* product.

Impressions & Clicks

There are so many ways to drive traffic to your listing on Amazon now compared to just a few years ago. A Brand Registered Third-Party Seller can now drive traffic with Sponsored Ads, Sponsored Brands (formerly called Headline Ads), Sponsored Display (retargeting ads off Amazon that bring traffic back to your listings), and Organic Traffic from great, Search Engine Optimized (SEO'd) listings. This is another place where your *Amazon Jungle Seller's Survival Guide* can be especially helpful, where direct response marketing strategies can be used to separate your product from the pack. In the next chapter, Rick will talk in depth about why direct-to-consumer brand-building strategies increase sales conversions on Amazon, using video, in particular, to promote product benefits, drive traffic, and close sales.

There are many more ways to drive traffic to your listing off Amazon. In my years as a Seller, I used e-mail, press releases, social media, blog content, pay-per-click ads, and landing pages, among other channels. And as Amazon continues to reward Sellers for building brands, the best place to drive off-Amazon traffic is to your Amazon Brand Page. In 2018,

Amazon released the Stores Insights dashboard to help its store owners monitor their store's effectiveness and performance metrics. By creating links with source tags on your off-Amazon channels, you can see how well that traffic is performing. In Chapter 10, Rick shares additional marketing strategies that focus on building your brand off-Amazon, with case studies on how specific tactics work to strengthen the brand *off* Amazon, while also increasing sales conversions *on* Amazon.

Amazon Business Reports are a great place to view important page views and unit session percentages or conversion rates. If page views are going up, but they are driving conversion rates down, then it's time to check out the quality of your traffic. I learned a painful lesson about social media traffic when I pushed thousands of clicks from social media directly to top-selling Amazon listings, only to watch the sales rank (and sales conversions) drop like a rock. I discovered that there was a lot of social media traffic coming from bots. And bots don't buy product. As soon as I cut the social media traffic, our conversion rates, sales, and ranking went back to normal. This is another reason why I now push social media traffic to the Amazon Brand Page. I learned the hard way that not all traffic is created equal. By going directly to the Amazon Brand Page, I could strip out the bots and non-relevant/non-qualified traffic to my listings. Remember when I said that Amazon's main focus, unlike Google and Facebook, is *the sale of items*? Merely generating traffic isn't enough to lift your Amazon rank and increase sales. That traffic must convert, and the better your listing converts to a sale (compared to your competitors), the more product you will sell.

Ship Fast (FBA Logistics)

In my time building a home recreation and home fitness brand, I shipped a lot of heavy items via freight that were too large to be eligible for FBA and therefore didn't have the coveted Prime Badge. If I had it to do all over again, I might not have gotten into the business of shipping 200 to

1,000-pound items. Instead, I would have focused my attention on products that were "FBA-able" because life is so much easier as an Amazon Seller when Amazon is handling the difficult job of picking, packing, and delivering on time.

WHEN EVERYTHING CLICKS

Reaching the top of the Best Seller Rank with a product you've designed is a really great feeling. I'd even go as far as calling it a "Seller's high." When you successfully apply the key steps from this *Seller's Survival Guide* for finding a great product, creating a great listing, and driving traffic that converts (with fast, on-time delivery), the improvement in sales can be exponential in scale. I've had sales jump from two to three a day to 200 to 300 a day, depending on the size and price point. As the sales and good product reviews roll in, your listing becomes formidable, and it becomes the standard by which other Sellers must measure themselves. Long-time Sellers call it The Flywheel Effect, a phrase borrowed from Jeff Bezos himself, when he scribbled this diagram on a napkin in 2001.

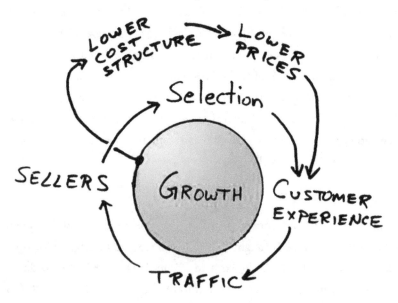

I recently sketched my own flywheel diagram for listings, and I keep it on my desk as a constant reminder of the winning formula on Amazon.

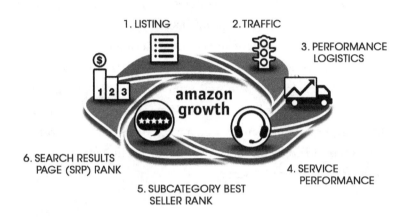

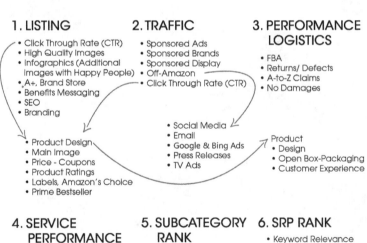

1. LISTING

- Click Through Rate (CTR)
- High Quality Images
- Infographics (Additional Images with Happy People)
- A+, Brand Store
- Benefits Messaging
- SEO
- Branding

- Product Design
- Main Image
- Price - Coupons
- Product Ratings
- Labels, Amazon's Choice
- Prime Bestseller

2. TRAFFIC

- Sponsored Ads
- Sponsored Brands
- Sponsored Display
- Off-Amazon
- Click Through Rate (CTR)

- Social Media
- Email
- Google & Bing Ads
- Press Releases
- TV Ads

3. PERFORMANCE LOGISTICS

- FBA
- Returns/ Defects
- A-to-Z Claims
- No Damages

Product
- Design
- Open Box-Packaging
- Customer Experience

4. SERVICE PERFORMANCE

- Seller Rating
- Product Rating Mangement
- Customer Service
- Customer Experience

5. SUBCATEGORY RANK

- Sales Velocity
- Sales History
- Product & Seller Ratings

6. SRP RANK

- Keyword Relevance
- SEO
- Click Through Rate (CTR), Unit Session Percentage (Conversions), and Sales Quantity
- Sales Velocity
- Product Ratings

I've shared a number of different metrics available from Amazon to help you manage your listings and to make changes for success.

Given everything Third-Party Sellers do for Amazon, I believe Amazon should be even more forthcoming in the data they provide to Sellers. Recently, in a Bloomberg TV interview, I said that if Amazon is going to use our data to knock off our products, then the least they can do is share the data they have on *our* products and product listings. I'm not asking for the customer names and contact information; that information belongs to Amazon. But each additional metric Amazon shares with Sellers only helps Sellers improve and do better. Regardless, if you focus on the metrics that I have laid out in this chapter, and you adjust things to improve your listings, I guarantee you'll be happy with the results. Amazon is difficult, but following the right strategy can help you beat them at their own game.

SECTION III:

Set yourself apart

Chapter 7:

BUILDING YOUR BRAND *ON* AMAZON

"MOST PEOPLE DO NOT LISTEN WITH THE INTENT TO
UNDERSTAND; THEY LISTEN WITH THE INTENT TO REPLY."

STEPHEN R. COVEY

I knew of Rick Cesari well before meeting him thanks to a common friend, Dr. Jeremy Weisz. Jeremy is the founder of INspired INsider, a popular podcast out of Chicago, where business owners and experts talk about their biggest business challenges and successes. Rick and I were guests on his podcast at separate times, and realizing that we both lived in Seattle, Jeremy encouraged each of us to reach out to the other and make a connection. At the time, Rick was advising clients about branding and marketing, but had relatively little experience selling on Amazon. Conversely, I knew Amazon from years in the trenches as a Seller, but I wasn't as familiar with the Direct-To-Consumer (DTC) techniques for which Rick was a master. In separate interviews, months apart, Jeremy realized that Rick was the yin to my yang. Plus, he had a hunch we'd become fast friends.

I was excited to meet Rick, but due to business commitments, I let time get away from me. It was a year or so later that we finally met when we were both invited by our mutual friend James Thomson to speak at the 2016 Prosper Show in Las Vegas. James had asked Rick to be the keynote speaker and to present on how to build winning brands. At the time, Sellers like me were cranking out listings, without much thought about branding, and we were making money at it. Getting items at low prices and listing them fast was the game back then and margins were a heck of a lot better than they are now. Many products at that time used price-cutting as a way to win the Buy Box, which triggers the "race-to-the-bottom" phenomenon I talked about in the first chapter. Having worked at Amazon for many years, James fully understood the impact price-cutting tactics have on 3P Sellers, and he created the Prosper Show to help them become more sophisticated in resisting the "Amazon squeeze." James viewed Rick—and his years of brand success through DTC marketing—as a positive role model for Amazon Sellers, and he believed Rick's expertise could really help Sellers build deeper relationships with their customers. I was especially grateful for Rick's appearance at the conference because it was my opportunity to make an overdue connection.

Everything Rick said in his 90-minute branding and marketing presentation that day hit me like a lightning strike. Just like the sudden burst of insight I experienced at the Klaristenfeld's dinner table, Rick's branding message sparked what I can only describe as a spontaneous understanding of what was missing from my own online selling strategy—*how* to build a brand. Rick was mobbed after his talk, so I caught him in the hallway later. I had so many questions! We exchanged business cards and we set a date to grab coffee the following Friday. It was the start of a weekly ritual that continues to this day, four years later, and it was a turning point in my entire approach to selling on Amazon.

BEST OF BOTH WORLDS

Over countless cups of coffee at the Issaquah Coffee Company, Rick shared his wealth of knowledge about the human psychology of selling. For more than 30 years, Rick has tested and refined his direct response methods for video and television commercials that made products like the Juiceman Juicer, George Foreman Grill, the Sonicare toothbrush, and GoPro cameras household names. I especially love how nonchalant Rick is when he talks about how he built one billion-dollar brand after another. It's part of what makes him accessible, as well as a great mentor. After a few of Rick's lessons, I tested some of his tactics on a handful of my Amazon listings. I was completely floored by the results. In some cases, sales increase by as much as 40% compared to my previous features-focused listings. None of this surprised Rick. While the technology may have changed dramatically since his first TV infomercial in 1989, the underlying principles of human psychology that drive purchasing behaviors are *exactly* the same today as they were then. In fact, the advances in technology, and a growing emphasis on social media as a way to connect with people, have actually made Rick's original brand-building formulas easier to implement and *even more relevant today.*

I'll give you an example. One of the first listings I showed Rick was of a ping pong table. I hadn't really thought about it then, but the listing copy read like a manufacturer's spec sheet, filled with jargon and other information that was dull and unrelated to the benefits of the table. I used graphics, but they called out the same features that surely put Amazon shoppers to sleep. The part that really got Rick fired up, though, was the video I'd included on the listing. It showed a couple of unhappy guys assembling my ping pong table. I know why I did that. I thought it would be really helpful to see how to put it together! But Rick's first comment to me was, "That looks like a lot of work." The lesson here that I've never forgotten was that when someone buys something, *they want to know the joy it brings, not the hard work involved up front.* While an assembly video has its place, and Rick would agree, it is something better shared *after* the actual purchase. To create a new video for my ping pong table listing, Rick connected me with a photographer and videographer who had direct response marketing experience. We found attractive, aspirational models, with great smiles, who played ping pong together "as a family." With these key changes, we turned our listing and messaging from a boring manufacturer's specification sheet into key benefits, with headlines like *Bring Friends and Family Together* and *Instructions: Play* and *Easily Folds for Storage When Not in Use.* These were the *benefits* shoppers were searching for, and with the addition of aspirational photos and video, sales increased by more than 50%. In retrospect, this all seems pretty obvious, but Rick helped me understand what motivates consumers to buy and how to better use those tools to promote a more compelling listing.

Jeremy Weisz's original hunch was spot on. What I was lacking in marketing knowledge, Rick had in abundance, and the reciprocating value of our unique experiences and compatible skill sets continue to help our clients across all of the retail channels—online and offline. In 2018, after my wife Ann received a job offer with Bristol-Myers Squibb, we moved the family to the opposite coast, transforming my Friday meetings with Rick from a casual chat at the coffee house to Friday morning Zoom meetings from Princeton, New Jersey. While web-conferencing technology can't replace the ambiance of a Seattle coffee house, Rick and I are more connected than ever, blending our strengths to help our shared clients improve their sales performances and build better brands

Rick's version

Before I met Jason, I'd caught a glimpse of the power of selling on Amazon when I was approached by two brothers who wanted to make an infomercial to grow their business. They were having a lot of success selling blenders online, moving about a container a month. At the time, there was no middle-range price for blenders. You could either get a cheap, underpowered blender (for under $100) or a high-end, powerful blender for $300+. The brothers had successfully carved out a niche in the middle-price range ($150) for a quality, powerful blender. I was impressed, and I was interested in their product because I had experience taking small product successes and growing them with direct response marketing campaigns. What further peaked my interest was that all of their sales were coming through Amazon. I remember thinking what kind of a platform can generate such a large amount of sales for an ordinary item like a blender? I'd been hearing other success stories like this one, and as a long-time DTC product marketer, I am always on the hunt for new sales channels.

Not long after the blender connection, our mutual friend James Thomson invited me to make the keynote address at the Prosper Show in Las Vegas. What an eye-opening experience that was! My presentation was on *The 5 Keys to Building A Great Brand*, which I'll share with you later in this chapter. At the conference, I shared real-life examples from product campaigns I'd worked on. I guess I was bringing the right message at the right time because I was mobbed afterwards by Amazon Sellers like Jason, looking for branding secrets to give them a competitive edge on the platform. Competition was heating up and Sellers realized they needed to be savvier marketers. I was fascinated by the stories I was hearing at the conference, including a young man doing more than $100,000 a month with a charcoal-based teeth cleaner; another generating more than $20,000 a month selling toasters. I distinctly remember meeting Jason and exchanging business cards. At the time he had a successful, eight-figure business called Dazadi. In a separate presentation at the same show, he talked about his method for finding successful products. He was also mobbed after his talk, and I was one of his admirers!

While I'd made a name for myself in marketing, I was new to Amazon. Jason was an Amazon Top Seller in his prime (no pun intended!), but he had more to learn about leveraging direct response marketing strategies to grow big brands. We were a perfect fit.

I looked forward to our first meeting back home. Issaquah is a small town about half-way between the two cities where Jason and I lived at the time. I'd conducted other meetings at the Issaquah Coffee Company and suggested it as a good spot for our first conversation. At the time I didn't realize there'd be many more get-togethers there before Jason relocated to New Jersey. We hit it off immediately as we are both product marketers at heart. Jason wanted all the information I could share about my product marketing successes; I wanted all the knowledge Jason had about selling on Amazon. Following is a recap of some of the lessons we shared over coffee—lessons we continue to draw from as we work together to help our clients grow sales and expand their brands.

FEATURES TELL, BENEFITS SELL.

I know this keeps coming up, but this time it's my turn to say it: *features tell; benefits sell.* Jason talks about it in terms of listing optimization in Chapter 5. He also shared his own aha moment at our first coffee meeting, when he showed me a product assembly video when he should have created an exciting demonstration video instead! Thirty years ago, I created the Juiceman Juicer at a time when popular brands like Braun and Krups were touting the quality German engineering features of their juice machines. These brands should have easily had an edge over a newcomer like me, but they made the same mistake most Sellers make. They focused on product features like stainless steel blades, a powerful motor, and dishwasher-safe plastic. When my company began marketing our juice machine, we took a totally different approach, focusing instead on the health benefits of drinking fresh juice, like weight loss, more energy, and healthier skin, nails, and hair. Positioning the product like this really helped increase sales exponentially, generating $75 million in sales for our company, Trillium Health Products, in just four years. While the competition was selling a sturdy kitchen appliance, we were selling a *health machine*!

Back to Jason's "aha moment." I knew right away that he was a natural brand-builder. The work he'd put into finding a great product was obvious; plus he knew how to set his products apart from the others, using fun, colorful designs, which really stood out against the boring monotones of the other products on the market. He just needed to prove to shoppers that he had what they were looking for. A quick-study, Jason took my advice and made a few simple changes, replacing dull photos with lifestyle shots of people having fun playing ping pong. It was a relatively easy change, with a major impact on sales. Leave the features for the spec sheets and talk about your product benefits where it counts most on Amazon—in your product listing and on your Amazon Brand Page.

READ THE REVIEWS

Jason has always relied on Amazon ratings to know whether or not he has a product with winning potential. As I learned more about his research process for finding winning products, I realized the obvious connection to how I built successful brands over the years—through authentic testimonials. I'd say testimonials are the primary reason for my marketing success. While Amazon doesn't permit the use of customer testimonials in their listings, they do provide all the feedback you need to be successful in the form of their customer ratings. I look at these reviews as a modern-day version of the focus group, but much better because the person providing the feedback is not being paid to tell you what they think. Amazon reviews come from real people, using your product and talking about their experience. That information is worth its weight in gold, as Jason explained in Chapter 3. It's how he builds a "better mousetrap" and it is how I've created winning brands for decades.

Prior to meeting Jason, my team used customer feedback with the George Foreman Grill to expand the product line. The original grill was small and could only cook four burgers. We added a six-burger grill, then an eight-burger grill. We eventually created an outside grill, plus added a timer and temperature controls *because that's what our customers wanted.* Their feedback (and our willingness and ability to respond) helped turn the grill into a billion-dollar brand. *Human behavior doesn't change, even when the message delivery platforms do.* When I was getting started, we used direct mail, then radio, then direct response television. Now it's Amazon, Facebook, and Instagram. If you understand the human psychology and some basic direct response marketing principles, these branding and marketing ideas will work on any platform.

SHARE YOUR BACKSTORY

To build a successful brand today, you've got to have an origin story. I love hearing how a company got started. If I think about my favorite products—the stuff in my house that I use in some form or fashion every day—I can tell you about the companies behind most of them. I know Jason has addressed this already, and it's something we tell our clients repeatedly—it's just not enough anymore to throw something up on Amazon and expect good results. You must distinguish yourself from the competition, and your origin story is one of the best places to start.

When Jason and I first start working with a new client, one of the first things we do is ask about the company's backstory. Telling your story is one of the most important, foundational steps a business can take to improve their sales and conversion rates. Why? People want to make connections. It's instinctual. The more you can share *who* you are, the more customers will trust *what* you are. There's a great book about this by Simon Sinek called *Start With Why.* I highly recommend it as a way to explore your own story and how it has influenced your business. Once you find and create your origin story, share it broadly—across every one of your marketing channels, with emphasis on using video whenever you can. Your story is your connection to your customer base, and that base will grow with you (and it will expand) because of the loyalty your personal story fosters.

Puriya: The ultimate origin story

Three years ago, I was invited to give a short presentation at a mastermind meeting in Seattle. This particular group was organized by Steve Simonson, a successful Amazon Seller, podcaster, and entrepreneur. As often happens after a group of ambitious business people get together, we mingle and network. Two young women stood out from the others. They were sisters, Jill and Yi-Jen, with a successful skin cream business. They approached me because they lacked brand awareness even though they had a terrific product. I asked them to tell me their story.

From Obscurity to Winner's Circle

Growing up in Taiwan, Jill and Yi-Jen used the power of plants every day. Their mother and grandmother had a botanical recipe for almost every ailment, and they grew up learning to look to nature first. When they moved to the United States, their mother was no longer there to simmer up potions and pastes the traditional way. Instead, the girls had to take care of themselves the "American way." When Jill needed medical treatment for a skin condition, she was shocked by the ingredients in her medications—drugs with 25-character ingredients that neither she nor Yi-Jen could even pronounce—and no natural options available.

Fast forward a few years and the sisters got to thinking: *What if our love of nature and our Mother's knowledge from home might help us find the solution to our own medical issues?* Despite their busy lives, they used every bit of spare time testing and researching natural, plant-based ingredients. By combining their educational backgrounds in science and research with their passion to help others, the sisters began to make progress.

They discovered that most of the hydrating creams and lotions used far too many bad chemicals. They had a small batch of their own cream manufactured, using their own unique formulation, and they tested it on themselves with great results. They also gave it to their close friends and family. They all loved it too! They decided to name it *The Mother of All Creams* as an homage to their mother and grandmother.

What a powerful origin story! We were able to use this on the new website. We also created new product images and added a scientific advisory board, all things that helped differentiate Puriya from the competition. Since re-launching the product, along with their origin story, Puriya has sold hundreds of thousands of units and was recently awarded the Family Tested, Family Approved seal of approval, sponsored by Parent Tested Parent Approved (ptpa.com).

If you're not currently using video on Amazon, then start. Can't afford a professional service? Use your smart phone and show people interacting with your product. This is one of the first things Jason and I advise our clients to do, and we consistently see increases in the sales conversions of as much as 20% or more. It's not all that surprising when you think about it. We are living in a video-first society now and technology allows everyone to create a video—simply and quickly. There's really no excuse not to use it in your marketing. Here are some eye-opening statistics I shared in my last book, *Video Persuasion*:

Using video in an email leads to 200-300% increase in click-through-rates.[16]

Social video generates 1,200% more shares than just text and image combined.[17]

---

[16] Colleen Davie Janes. "Video Is No Longer An Accessory for Marketing: Here's What You Need to Know," Forbes. December 15, 2016. https://www.forbes.com/sites/ellevate/2016/12/15/video-is-no-longer-a-marketing-accessory/#999096fde87a

[17] William Arruda. "Why You Need to Excel at Video," Forbes. June 29, 2016. https://www.forbes.com/sites/williamarruda/2016/06/29/why-you-need-to-excel-at-video/#530add5141c2

72% of customers would rather learn about a product or service by way of video.[18]

Putting it all together: The Plugable Story

A great example of how to incorporate many of the lessons shared in this chapter comes from Plugable Technologies, a company founded by my good friend, Bernie Thompson. Plugable sells many products in the highly competitive computer peripherals category, where margins are thin and competition is fierce. Yet he is an Amazon Top 200 Seller and the largest seller of docking stations on Amazon, enjoying year over year growth since launching on Amazon more than 11 years ago. How does he do it?

Plugable has been consistent in the use of video since day one. Every time Plugable launches a new product, they make a demonstration video explaining the benefits of the product. They use these videos on their Amazon listings, but they also post them on their Plugable YouTube channel. In addition, they create tutorial videos on how to use each of their products. These videos not only help sell the product, they also reduce the number of customer service issues. They also have a great origin story (also recorded on video) available on the Plugable website and on their Amazon Brand Page. In the video, Bernie talks about why he started the business and what you can expect when you buy a product from his company. This puts a human face behind the company, helping buyers feel more like they're buying from someone they know rather than a stranger. Plugable also has a great tag line: *Better products, better knowledge, and better service.* When you are selling products that are commodities, this service-oriented philosophy helps set Plugable apart from the competition. Listening to your customers and responding to their needs is a great way to garner respect and launch ahead on Amazon.

---

18   Adam Hayes. "The State of Video Marketing in 2020 [New Data]," Biteable. https://biteable.com/blog/video-marketing-statistics/

5 KEY STRATEGIES FOR BUILDING A GREAT BRAND

I mentioned that the topic of my presentation at the Prosper Show, where Jason and I first met, was on *The 5 Key Strategies for Building a Great Brand*. I'd recently published a book on brand-building, and the conference founder felt strongly that these strategies could really benefit 3P Sellers. Here are highlights from the presentation:

Key #1: Find your Unique Selling Proposition (USP)

I love to start with one of my favorite business quotes from Sally Hogshead, author of *Fascinate: How to Make Your Brand Impossible to Resist*. In it she writes, *Different is better than better*. Think about that. While most people are trying to incrementally increase how much better their product is than their competitors, Sally is suggesting you look for a way to differentiate your product from the others so that you have an open territory all of your own. Your Unique Selling Proposition (USP) is critical when determining how you can differentiate your product from all the other products in the marketplace. I'll use a real example. When I was working with Philips on their new Sonicare toothbrushes, the company was facing the steep challenge of trying to sell a $150 toothbrush in the marketplace where the next highest price was around $3. I came up with a really powerful USP that helped us break through the cost barrier: *Sonicare cleans beyond the bristles*. With our USP in place, we were able to leverage the sonic technology into *that something* no other toothbrush had. We included education in our messaging about how gum disease starts and how hidden bacteria (that other toothbrushes can't reach) is the cause. *Cleaning beyond the bristles* was quickly accepted as a major benefit and sales skyrocketed.

Key #2: Zig when they zag

There's another great book I like to reference called *The Blue Ocean Strategy*. Authors W. Chan Kim and Renee Mauborgne argue that lasting success comes from carving out your own space. In other words, *zig* when everybody else *zags*. I especially love the title of this book because it's so easy to visualize this wide open space where you want to be—the blue ocean. I'll share another example of how a former client of mine exemplifies this strategy. When I first met Nick Woodman, founder of GoPro, he was selling a new kind of camera out of the back of his van at the 2011 Outdoor Retailer Show in Salt Lake City. At the time there were many great cameras on the market, products from large companies, like Sony and Panasonic, with great camera technology. But Nick had a totally different idea, focused instead on the "action camera" segment of the marketplace where no one else was. He found the "blue ocean" and easily dominated this category on the way to becoming a billion-dollar company in just eight years.

Another dramatic example of how positioning—or *repositioning*— matters is in the case of the George Foreman Grill. That product originally came out of something called the Fajita Express. Ever heard of it? Exactly my point. Like the winning product in the end, the Fajita Express had the same slanted grill concept, but the reason for the slant was for sliding grilled meat into a taco shell. With my friends at Salton Appliances, I was asked to help re-think the purpose of the slant technology. And so it was renamed *The Lean, Mean, Fat-reducing Grilling Machine* with the tagline: "knock out the fat." The re-imagined grill went on to sell more than any other product in housewares' history, over 120 million units to date.

Key #3: Deliver Value

When you're building a brand you must always deliver value. I always tell clients to *under* promise and *over* deliver. You've got to exceed your customers' expectations wherever you can. A good example of this comes from the OxiClean brand. At the time my agency was running Direct Response TV ads featuring pitchman Billy Mays. When people ordered directly from our TV ads or online, they thought they were getting a 12 ounce tub of OxiClean. But when we delivered the product, we shipped a supersized tub instead. We also included samples of additional OxiClean products, like Orange Glo furniture polish, Orange Clean degreaser, or Kaboom tub and tile cleaner. People were always pleasantly surprised when they first opened their package! This allowed us to increase the perceived value a customer received, while also marketing new products, leading to potential future sales. Everybody wins! Richard Branson has a great philosophy about value, captured in this quote: "The key is to set realistic customer expectations and then exceed them, preferably in unexpected and helpful ways." Clearly this concept works, helping Branson build his hugely successful Virgin Brand.

Key #4: ALWAYS Listen to your Customers

For Jason, customer feedback is the pivotal information that helps him determine how to pick a winning product. I've used it for three decades to build enduring brands. In addition to listening to customer feedback to improve our products over the years, we both believe in delivering exceptional customer service. Now as consultants, we coach our clients to do the same. Great customer service helps company's build long-term relationships with their customers. In turn, this good will generates brand loyalty and allows companies to introduce new products down the line. Sales consultant David Forman said that customer service is an attitude, not a department. I believe that wholeheartedly and encouraged Sellers at the Prosper Show not to take any shortcuts in regard to listening (and responding) to what your customers have to say. Zappos.com is such a great example of a company discovering how to take customer complaints about shipping costs and delays and doing something totally different. They waived their shipping fees and charges for returns. This was a big gamble for Zappos, but the loyalty they generated by the service they were providing to their customers far outweighed the costs, eventually leading to their sale to Amazon for more than a billion dollars! Remember the Plugable example? This service-first philosophy builds trust and keeps customers coming back for more.

Key #5: Use Authentic Testimonials

Authentic product testimonials are one of the most powerful marketing tools you can use to sell your products. Every e-commerce site could improve sales and conversion by simply adding real user-testimonials. This concept has worked for generations in every type of advertising vehicle ever used. I call it *timeless marketing*! Testimonials work well for three primary reasons:

Overcoming objections. People want to believe a product will work for them, but they usually have a list of objections for why it might not be the best fit. When they see or hear a testimony from someone else, it helps break down their own objections and remove barriers to purchase.

Establishing credibility. People will believe your advertising and product marketing *if they believe it is credible.* Testimonials are a great way to establish credibility. I like to use an expert for these types of testimonials, like a doctor or nurse if I'm selling a health product; a dentist or periodontist for oral care; a dermatologist for beauty products; and a chef for cooking products. Starting to get the idea?

Social Proof. In his book *Influence: The Psychology of Persuasion*, Dr. Robert Cialdini introduces the concept of *social proof.* Based in deep, human psychological behavior patterns, social proof says that when a person is in a situation where they don't know how to react, they will follow the lead of others. Applied to marketing, if someone is trying to make a decision about whether or not to buy your product, they will look for social proof before making the purchase. Amazon reviews are a great example of social proof. This is certainly not a new concept, as P.T. Barnum once said, "Nothing draws a crowd quite like a crowd." Amazon uses testimonials in every product listing, but they call them reviews. A product cannot succeed on Amazon without loads of five-star reviews. Whether you call them testimonials or reviews, they play the same powerful marketing role with every successful DTC brand.

AN AMAZON MAKE-OVER: THE VESTA PRECISION STORY

Whenever I have a new client, I start by asking Jason to check out the Amazon listings for their products. There is usually room for improvement, and I engage Jason and his Avenue7Media team for an Amazon makeover. I have found this to be the absolute fastest way to increase sales for a consumer-goods business. Let's take a look at one client I brought to Jason, and how he helped them dramatically improve their Amazon sales.

Vesta Precision has gone from nowhere to everywhere, and the future is bright for their brand of sous vide cooking machines, vacuum sealers and bags. When I first started working with them, Amazon was an afterthought, and they had one poor guy trying to manage their Amazon business, as well as their e-commerce website and umpteen other channels. When Jason stepped in, he started by rescuing some of their suspended listings. Then he applied his tested method for Amazon success, starting with bad reviews and the customers' reasons behind them. Jason and his team then went to work on recrafting the brand's message, with a focus on the key benefits of the products that made the sous vide machines and accessories so special. For example, the Immersa Elite product is a small, foldable, powerful sous vide machine unlike any other product in its category. Not only is it cute, but it does the job of the larger machines; plus, it's really easy for home cooks to store in a kitchen drawer. Jason also identified the six highest-volume, most-relevant keywords, using them to recreate messaging for all of Vesta's listings. These benefits-focused messages were repeated in the images they provided to help shoppers visualize the benefits being called out. Finally, Jason and his team began the lengthy process of driving traffic, with Amazon Ads and other tools.

In short order, he helped a company that was doing nothing on Amazon become a 7-figure Seller in about a year.

Meeting Jason at the Seller's conference four years ago led to a successful business relationship and a lasting friendship. In this chapter we looked at the ways in which that relationship has benefitted our businesses and helped our clients grow sales by building authentic brands. In Chapter 10, I'll talk about effective strategies for expanding your business off-Amazon and how a strong presence, across multiple marketing channels, actually improves your performance *on* Amazon.

CHAPTER SUMMARY

- With more than 600 million products on Amazon U.S. (and growing), building your brand on Amazon is essential for growing sales and fostering customer loyalty. In this chapter, Rick shared highlights from his *5 Key Strategies for Building a Great Brand,* and used examples he shared with Amazon Sellers at the 2016 Prosper Show, where he first met Jason Boyce.

- Rick shares his reflections on meeting Jason and how their complementary skill sets have brought them together as business partners and friends. Rick uses personal examples and case studies to illustrate some of the most successful direct response marketing strategies he has used over 30 years, creating billion-dollar brands that have endured the test of time.

- Rick shows how these same branding and direct response strategies translate perfectly to Amazon.

- Applying Direct-To-Consumer (DTC) branding strategies will increase your sales conversions on Amazon—guaranteed!

- Consumers want answers and a successful DTC campaign delivers with its focus on benefits, not features.

- Rick's focus on building relationships for the long-term complement Amazon's customer-first philosophy and inspired Jason to adopt Rick's marketing approach, which includes these 5 key brand-building tactics:
  1. *Find your Unique Selling Proposition*
  2. *Zig when they zag*
  3. *Deliver value*
  4. *Always listen to your customer*
  5. *Use authentic testimonials*

- A comprehensive DTC campaign includes off-Amazon marketing, which will be explored in more depth in Chapter 10.

Chapter 8:

FULFILLMENT & INVENTORY

I n this book, I have laid out what I believe is the best way to survive and in fact thrive on Amazon—as a Private-Label Seller. I'll circle back to some of the merits of the private label model at the end of this chapter, but I wanted to touch on some of the different ways people sell on Amazon, some of which I've tried and done successfully. That said, Amazon has made many changes over the years that make these alternatives more difficult to pull off than in years past.

RETAIL ARBITRAGE

Retail arbitrage is a fairly simple concept and there are a ton of

Amazon Sellers running successful business on Amazon in this way. While I'm not a big fan, it's a great way for a person just starting out to get their feet wet selling other people's brands. A retail arbitrageur buys products from a retail store or a distributor at deep discounts and then sells them through online marketplaces, like Amazon, for a profit. This is the cleanest way to do Retail Arbitrage; however, there is another way that frustrates old Private-Label Sellers like me. I talked earlier about how Amazon makes it easy for other Sellers to attach to existing Amazon listings. This is how they built the Buy Box System. But some retail arbitrageurs will attach to your listing and offer your item at a much higher price. They'll even get the sale if the main Seller is out of stock or doesn't have inventory to fulfill the order from a certain part of the country. When an Amazon customer buys from one of these Sellers, the retail arbitrageur simply buys the product from the main Seller when it is back in stock and ships it directly to their customer.

Have a look at this screenshot. There is only one authorized Seller of this brand, BetterYou. The other two listings in this Buy Box are retail arbitrageurs.

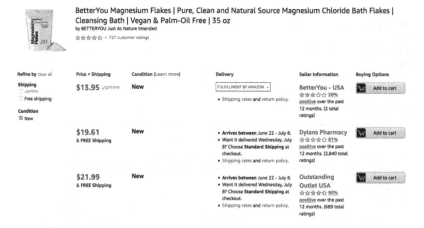

If you're a good bargain hunter, and you understand the true market retail prices for items, then this can be a fruitful way to test the market on Amazon. It's not that I don't understand it. I just can't understand why someone would do business this way when it doesn't take much effort to identify brands and buy them at wholesale prices. Additionally, this can be a very frustrating way to do business on Amazon when and if the brands that you are selling become gated by Amazon, thus blocking *you* from selling them. It can also open the door to legal action by the brand against the Seller. Getting a legal notice from a brand, or being stuck with inventory you can no longer sell, are two big reasons why this isn't a great option, in my opinion.

DROPSHIPPING

Dropshipping is a just-in-time (JIT) inventory method near and dear to my heart. If it wasn't for dropshipping, I never would have been able to build an eight-figure business on Amazon. With dropshipping, you simply list an item, sell it, and have your vendor or distributor directly ship that item to your customer. When done properly, and given the right kind of market, dropshipping requires very little cash flow, and it can allow a Seller to scale and grow quickly.

In theory, it's a great way to start out. But Amazon has made it increasingly difficult for dropshippers to survive, including officially banning the practice for Amazon Sellers.

When I was first starting out in 2002, my brothers and I were dropshipping everything we could get our virtual hands on, adding tens of thousands of products to our website by the end of 2010. The hardest part was convincing a vendor or distributor to ship one item at a time, rather than pallets or truckloads as they were accustomed to doing. But once we had them convinced, life was good. In 2002 we did $100,000 in sales; the next year we did $1,000,000. By 2004 we were selling $2,000,000 a year in product. This level of scalability wouldn't normally have been possible without large amounts of capital or financing, but dropshipping allowed us to grow without either. That is until Amazon came along and raised the bar for deliveries to customers.

These three metrics essentially killed dropshipping on Amazon: (1) Late Shipping Rate (LSR), (2) Pre-fulfillment Cancel Rate (PCR), and (3) Order Defect Rate (ODR). When these metrics top 4 percent, 2.5 percent, and 1 percent respectively, Amazon suspends your account. I know this because that is exactly what happened to my business in 2013. After we learned why our account was suspended, we began a rapid change to carrying inventory for other brands, and we doubled-down on a strategy we'd been working on for years—grow our own brands.

Before Prime Delivery, no one really knew they *needed* free, 2-Day shipping. Now we can't live without it. Consequently, a dropship method that relies on wholesalers to meet your customers' needs, simply doesn't work. No matter how many software systems my brothers and I engineered to manage this process, and regardless of our carefully-constructed contracts with suppliers, no one else could reliably perform the way Amazon demanded. If our supplier promised to ship in a day, they typically wouldn't ship for five (LSR). If they promised to keep our items fully stocked, we'd hear three days later that they were out of stock, which would require us to cancel the order before it shipped (PCR). If our customer ordered a red one and the vendor shipped a blue one, our ODR would go up. Don't get me wrong, all of these issues are very important. I know I demand them from e-commerce companies when I buy things. In fact I'd say Amazon made me a better Seller by raising the bar for better overall customer service. However, a "heads up" would've been really helpful before suspending my account and cutting off my cash flow. Like most things Amazon, sudden changes like this can be catastrophic to 3P Sellers.

CARRYING OTHER PEOPLE'S INVENTORY

In the early days, we only purchased inventory from brands that wouldn't dropship to our customers, stuff we considered integral to our brand's overall success. For example, we carried an inventory of Spalding basketballs because Spalding wouldn't dropship them, and you can't have a very good basketball store without the official game ball of the National Basketball Association. So we sucked it up, and we bought and stored basketballs. Over time we expanded our inventoried items until eventually moving to an all-inventory model after Amazon dropped that surprise suspension on us in 2013 for bad order metrics.

If you're going to purchase other people's inventory, then I highly recommend the following strategy: Ask your supplier for unique or exclusive products to sell—products where you alone are the exclusive Seller with a specific product and a unique UPC code. This is a very effective way to be the *Only Seller in the Buy Box*; plus you can create better listings and potentially offer your item at a higher price than the other guys. Why? Because your item is unique, different, and exclusive. This strategy worked for us, and it is still a solid Amazon strategy today.

If you're just starting out, it may be difficult to come up with the cash for an order size large enough for a vendor to offer you an exclusive item, but there is another way. We noticed that when we owned *all* of the inventory for a given SKU, and we didn't share the Buy Box with any other Sellers, then we consistently sold 10 times the sales volume compared to our other listings where we shared the Buy Box. We stumbled onto this idea when we started purchasing the last remaining inventory of close-out items from our suppliers. The only downside was that as the listing gained sales rank, we were unable to restock it because there was nothing left. That's when we began working with our suppliers to create unique exclusive products just for us.

As long as a vendor protects your exclusivity and doesn't sell it to others behind your back, exclusive items can boost your sales and add to your protective moat on Amazon. Taking charge of your own inventory, either by sending it to FBA or shipping it out of your own warehouse with FBM (Fulfillment by Merchant) listings, also guarantees that your order metrics will remain strong, helping you avoid painful suspensions. To this day, having exclusives is the safest way to sell other people's products on Amazon.

YOUR OWN PRIVATE LABEL

Although exclusive rights to carry someone else's brand, while also managing the inventory, are two giant leaps forward, neither will get you to a Top-Seller ranking (or top-profit margins) on Amazon. By far the best way to sell on Amazon is to create and sell your own private label brand of product with the methods we've shared in this book. Private label products are those manufactured by you or your contract factory and sold under your own proprietary and trademark-protected brand name. Owning your own brand can almost guarantee you will own your own Buy Box, and you can build a lasting legacy as well. When you create your own brand, you control your story. You have the freedom to create your own look and feel, around which you can market to consumers on (and off) the Amazon.com platform. I've absolutely loved my journey of creating my own brands and growing them.

FULFILLMENT BY AMAZON (FBA)

In Chapter 4, I regaled you with the advantages of Fulfillment by Amazon (FBA). I called it your very own Good Housekeeping seal of approval because when you sign up for FBA your product earns the hallowed Prime Badge. Whether you are a retail arbitrageur, reseller, or Private Label Seller, it goes without saying that the best way to store, pick, pack, and ship on Amazon is with FBA. You sell it. They ship it. Put frankly, if eBay had used its considerable wealth to build and execute an FBA-like fulfillment network for its Sellers 15 years ago, I'd be writing about how to sell on eBay right now rather than Amazon. FBA gives you scalability. When your product lands and you go from selling one a day to 1,000, Amazon can accommodate that higher daily volume without you having to hire staff or find a larger warehouse space. Fulfillment by Amazon is a big reason why Amazon won e-commerce.

While I strongly recommend FBA for even the most experienced Amazon Sellers, there is also no better way for new Amazon Sellers to get started. Besides becoming your fulfillment center, there are a number of additional advantages, including low cost, especially for smaller-packaged items. Through FBA, Amazon fully supports your growth and handles some of the customer service issues, like returns. Of course those "extras" come at an additional cost, but with FBA you can avoid expensive rent, additional payroll costs, like workers' comp, and other fees associated with doing it yourself. This is especially important if you have a seasonal business because you won't have to pay for empty space in the off season; you just pay for what you use. But as I said earlier, the best reason to FBA is the coveted Prime Badge, which can give you a 30%+ lift in sales. In my experience, FBA is safe, it's scalable, it's cost-effective, and it helps you focus on what's most important—listening to your customers and using that information to make your products and listings better.

Amazon currently does not offer FBA for large, oversized items, but they are working on it. Unfortunately, for oversized items, the only option is for Sellers to warehouse and ship individual orders themselves through Fulfilment by Merchant (FBM). If Amazon had offered FBA for large items like pool tables or air hockey tables, I might still be selling those items myself. Working with a multitude of Less Than Truckload (LTL) shippers and a third-party warehouse to hold large inventory is not something I miss. It was painfully time-consuming and hard to manage. We ultimately did a great job delivering for our customers, but I wouldn't want to do it again.

FBA Onsite is a new program that Amazon is currently beta-testing with select Sellers. This program basically turns a portion of your own warehouse operations into mini FBA centers, complete with Amazon software, equipment and sometimes—even staff! I'll be tracking the progress of this new venture that could well become the next frontier in ways to store, pick, pack, and ship your Amazon orders. Amazon is always exploring new ways to expand capacity, without losing control of their ever-important orders metrics—All this while someone else pays the rent.

I've enjoyed writing this chapter about the different ways I grew my Amazon business over the years. I sometimes miss those early dropship days, when I first discovered that exclusive products could outperform everything else I was selling. Upon reflection, I am reminded of the incredible speed by which the Amazon supply chain network of warehousing, fulfillment, and delivery has grown over the years. It wasn't that long ago they only had four warehouses! Staying informed on fulfillment options is an important part of your Amazon success, and don't shy away from new programs as they roll out, like FBA Onsite, when it's available. While Amazon is ultimately looking for its own competitive advantage, the improvements it makes in the areas of shipping and fulfilment typically benefit Sellers too. Getting in early can give you a leg up on the competition.

CHAPTER SUMMARY

- While having your own private label brand is the best way to build a brand on Amazon, there are several alternative strategies for Sellers, including retail arbitrage, dropshipping, and carrying other people's inventory.

- Success using these alternative selling strategies is harder to achieve largely because Amazon is so good at what it does best—offering products at low prices and delivering them reliably in a day or two.

- The absolute safest way to have success on Amazon is to create your own trademarked brand and make it great. This way you own the Buy Box, and you build brand-equity that can serve you well, if you ever decide to sell your company.

- Use Amazon's Fulfillment by Amazon (FBA) network for that Prime Badge advantage, which can help grow your sales by as much as 30%.

Chapter 9:

PAY TO PLAY!

I have a love-hate relationship with Amazon Advertising. On one hand, Amazon Sponsored Ads can really help drive traffic, sales, and search relevancy to products using targeted keywords. On the other, these ads are based on a cost-per-click (CPC) basis and competitive bidding constantly drives up CPCs. When Amazon launched its sponsored products advertising program in 2013, the CPC was small, as low as five cents per click. By 2020, CPCs for high-volume keywords were as high as $17 per click—and that's not a typo!

In 2002, my brothers and I were paying for clicks to drive search engine traffic to SuperDuperHoops.com through a company called Overture. Overture pioneered pay-per-click (PPC) advertising, and it was later bought by Yahoo. Yahoo licensed the technology to Google, where they perfected PPC in what they now call Google Ads. In a few short years, the CPC to drive search traffic to our e-commerce site jumped from a nickel a click to $5, and we quickly realized that this same scenario would play out on Amazon as well. I was right. In the end, I believe sponsored ads will drive up prices on Amazon, perhaps beyond Mr. Bezos' comfort level. For now, they are a necessary evil, and also one of the fastest-changing segments on Amazon. By the time you read this chapter, I'm certain some of the ad types, as well as the user interface for managing Amazon Ads, will have changed. For that reason, this chapter will focus more on basic terminology and ad placement, followed by proper strategy for ad management.

WHY ARE ADS SO IMPORTANT?

It all goes back to keywords and phrases in a product listing for organic search results. If you're not on the first or second page of Amazon Search Results, you simply won't get noticed. You also won't get clicks. And you definitely won't get sales. Amazon Ads allow your product to rank higher in search results when shoppers search for products. Good ad placement helps your product get seen and get sales, and because Amazon's algorithm likes sales more than anything else, it rewards you with better placement. When a paid keyword ad converts to a sale for your listing, the search algorithm adds relevance, and it links that keyword to your product. If you get enough sales driven by that keyword, then Amazon's search ranking algorithm will not only give your ads better placement for less money, it will also help your product rank in the organic search results. Organic rank is important because those clicks are free and the more organic sales a Seller gets, the more that Seller can afford to buy more ads, which doubles their presence on search results. If you can rank high on the Page 1 with an organic link *and* a sponsored link, then you've just doubled your chances of getting the click.

4 TYPES OF AMAZON ADVERTISING

It's Pay to Play on Amazon today. For virtually every product search conducted, the majority of above-the-fold space comes from *paid advertising*. Check out the Amazon Search Results Page for my favorite two keywords, "water bottles." Of the 65 products listed, 12 are Sponsored Ads. While there is some variation in the layout based on categories, the majority that appear above the fold are sponsored. Paying to play is your best chance of getting seen, and being seen is everything.

As of the writing of this book, the following are types of PPC Amazon Ads available to Third-Party Sellers:

Sponsored Brands. S'well is paying for a Sponsored Brand Ad, formerly known as Headline Search Ads (HSA), and they take up the top section of all search results. A click on a Sponsored Brand Ad may take you to the brand's Amazon Brand Store or it could take you to a listings page loaded with the brand's products.

Sponsored Ads. In the image above, Takeya Actives is running the sole Sponsored Ad, but many times Sponsored Ads will take up the entire first row of search results. Sponsored Ads can be set to display based on keywords, a competitor's product or ASIN, a product category, or a competitor's brand name. If a Seller has deep pockets they can literally block out their competitors' ad space.

Sponsored Display. Display Ads are relatively new to Campaign Manager (2019). They allow the Seller to serve banner ads on Amazon's large inventory of displays ads (virtual billboards), both on and off Amazon. Display Ads are powered by Amazon DSP and are sold on a cost-per-click basis. Prices can vary depending on format and placement. If you pay for display ads, you may also find your ad follows you when you leave Amazon to check the news on CNN.com or your favorite team on ESPN. That particular ad is a retargeting ad. We've had mixed results with Sponsored Display Ads, but for some clients it's a winner.

Amazon DSP. Demand Side Platform is a programmatic way to reach audiences. The power of DSP is not necessarily that it serves banner ads and product videos to the exact type of customer that buys your products; rather, it does the opposite. If a customer has already purchased your product, then DSP *does not serve ads* to your type of customer. That is the DSP superpower. In the first chapter, I shared that *Facebook knows what you like, Google knows what you search, but Amazon knows what you buy*. It is Amazon's ability to know what customers buy that makes their form of digital advertising more potent than Facebook's and Google's, especially when it comes to the sale of physical products. Amazon DSP ads are sold on a cost-per-thousand impressions basis, and the minimum ad spend to qualify for these kind of ads can reach $35,000 for 60 days of impressions.

Our agency doesn't do a lot of Amazon DSP campaigns because, frankly, the return on investment hasn't been as favorable as with other sponsored ad-types. But DSP is being increasingly used by big national brands for brand awareness campaigns. Think television or billboard ads, where it's difficult to measure whether that ad drove a direct sale. The goal of DSP display ad placement is to drive brand awareness. If it drives sales too, then great, but it's not the end-goal of DSP. Helping a brand gain "mind share" *is* the goal. It's hard to go anywhere online these days without seeing Amazon ads and, increasingly, Amazon is reselling that space to brands. Look out Facebook and Google, Amazon Ads has you in their sights.

KEEP YOUR EYE ON THE BALL

Like with most goals, measuring success is important for tracking your progress. No matter what kind of marketing you are doing, keeping your eye on key metrics and adjusting accordingly is an absolute must. The Campaign Manager in Seller Central offers many important ad metrics, and I would argue that tracking them on a daily basis can mean the difference between Amazon success and bankruptcy. Following are just a basic tools I recommend you keep at the top of your daily checklist:

Impressions. An impression is a pay-per-click metric that reveals how often your ad is appearing on Amazon. It is possible for impressions to be overlooked, but if the ad is served on the screen while a shopper is viewing the search results page, for example, then it's likely the ad or product was seen. Impressions are important because, if they are consistently low, it signifies that the particular keyword you are using is not very popular and you'll want to consider using another keyword that attracts more "eyeballs."

Clicks. When an ad is served and a shopper sees it and "clicks" on your ad or product, you are that much closer to closing the sale. Clicks are good, but if you're paying for ads by-the-click then you want to make sure that a healthy number of those paid clicks convert to sales. If not, your spending can skyrocket, and you'll start losing money.

Click-Through-Rate (CTR). This is the ratio of shoppers who click on your ad or product compared to the number of shoppers who were served or who saw your ad or product. When your CTR is low on Amazon it could mean that your image, price, reviews, or product title are not as attractive as your competitors. When CTR is low, it is important to test new and better images and update your title so that your listing stands out on the crowded SRP. Click-through-rates can also be positively affected by good product design that is cool, distinctive, and grabs a viewer's attention.

Cost-Per-Click (CPC). The amount you pay for each click to your product is the CPC. If you are paying a lot for clicks, and you get shoppers to click through to your product, you want to be sure those clicks convert to sales. In Chapter 5 we discussed how to create listings that sell in order to help clicks convert to sales.

Ad Spend. The total dollar amount spent on ads is your ad spend, which can get as high as $20,000 per month for just one product. This may seem daunting at first, but if I told you this product was also producing $250,000 in sales each month, I'll bet you'd find the total ad spend a lot easier to swallow. This is the reason why my firm focuses on TACoS (see below) for the best metric to grow profitably

Ad Cost of Sales (ACoS). Before we skip ahead to my favorite metric (TACoS), let's take a quick look at ACoS, a somewhat controversial metric. ACoS tells you what percentage of your ad sales is going towards the ad spend. The attribution window for Sponsored Ads is only seven days, so a sale gets attributed to an ad or an ad sale within seven days of the first ad click. It is for this reason that I don't really like this metric. If a shopper clicks now, but comes back in eight days to buy your product, there is no way of knowing that the first click came from the ad. This is why I prefer the TACoS metric because the last thing you want to do is cut a keyword that drove that first click on Day 1, then converted it shortly thereafter, but not fast enough for ACoS.

TACoS or Overall ACoS. This is my favorite performance metric because it assesses the impact of advertising relative to Amazon sales. Plus the name is catchy, for which I give my friends at Teikametrics credit. At Avenue7Media, we set monthly goals for sales growth and TACoS, and I personally check *both* metrics daily for each of my clients' products. The TACoS goal depends on the size of your profit margin. Products with a 50% profit margin may be able to afford a 30% TACoS. Comparatively, products with a 5% margin can't afford much by way of ads or TACoS at all. Also, the TACoS goal we start with at launch is much higher than our long-term TACoS goal, which tapers off as the performance of the ad campaign improves through optimization.

CAST A WIDE NET

Campaign structure and flow can vary widely, and we typically create campaigns for every ASIN and/or product we advertise. We also create a flow that works from the time a product launches until the end of that product's life cycle. Here's a short list of my go-to campaign types:

Automatic Campaigns, where Amazon selects the keywords for your product. This is a great way to harvest keywords when first starting a campaign.

Manual Campaigns, where you pick keywords based on an Exact Match, Broad Match, or Phrase Match. Exact Match is restrictive, only driving traffic to the exact keyword you enter. Broad Match can be expensive because it serves any variation of your main keyword, which is why I prefer Phrase Match. This is a cost-effective, flexible alternative—but only if it performs better than the other two. That's right, test all three and stick with the one that works best for *your* products.

Sponsored Brand Campaigns can contain several keywords with different match types. If you're doing any kind of digital marketing or TV advertising, I highly recommend setting up Sponsored Brand Campaigns with your brand name keywords to make it as easy as possible for shoppers who see your television ad to go to their phone app to buy your brand on Amazon. Otherwise your ads are just driving sales to your competitors on Amazon.

When we launch a product ad, we start by creating an *Automatic Campaign* that includes a number of similar products as unique ad groups. Creating unique ad groups gives my team granularity, where we can easily track which keywords (or ASIN keywords) convert for given products. Conversely, putting all products or several products into one ad group makes it nearly impossible to tell which keyword converted for which product. For example, you may keep one keyword for one product that is converting to a sale and negate the same keyword for a different product that does not convert, thus saving ad spend. Creating unique ad groups allows you to fine-tune your ad spend so that you are only spending on what converts to sales.

We create our campaigns and ad groups in a way that casts a wide net in order to capture as many good, relevant keywords as possible. Amazon drives traffic via automatic campaigns from keywords auto-generated by its system. Some of those keywords convert to a sale; others do not. If by 20 to 50 clicks a keyword hasn't converted into a sale, it probably never will. That's when we negate it or make it a negative keyword, which signals Amazon to stop sending us traffic from that keyword.

When a keyword does convert to a sale, or several sales, we move that keyword into a *Manual Campaign.* Manual campaigns can include an exact match for that keyword or a phrase match, where the phrase stays the same but an additional keyword is added either before or after the phrase. Broad match campaigns allow for the reordering of keyword phrases, which allows only traffic that is most relevant to your product to continue to be sent. At the launch of a new product we fully expect to lose money on every sale for up to six weeks while we cast this wide net of keywords searches for those with the highest-conversion rates on which to double-down.

Here are the TACoS metric goals for the first six months of a typical product launch:

Month 1	100%
Month 2	75%
Month 3	50%
Month 4	35%
Month 5	25%
Month 6	5—25%*

*Based on profit margins

Although this wide-net strategy can be painful to bootstrapped entrepreneurs, it is important in the training of the Amazon Search Algorithm to recognize your product and grant you the prime digital real estate it deserves on the platform. Build up your ad budget war chest prior to launch. Remember, your Amazon listings are an investment. After your products gain relevance and rank, you can put them on the balance sheet.

AD OPTIMIZATION

I've just described some of the high-level metrics, but there are many more levels and variations that successful advertising managers can use. While this is not an ad management book, these tips on ad management flow can help you focus on what's most important. My team starts with this same process and adjusts according to the category, the competition, and our clients' needs. Cast a wide net. Negate keywords that don't convert to sales. And double-down on those that do. Don't think for a moment that you can forget about these metrics once your campaigns are optimized. Keywords are fickle. In fact, Google regularly reports that as many as 15% of all searches have *never been done before*. The things that people search for, and the ways in which they conduct their searches, change more than you can imagine. For this reason, every month, my team runs a broad or automatic campaign for short bursts of time to capture new keywords for our optimized Manual Campaigns. This cyclical process ensures we are continually adding to our stable of solid keywords that grow sales.

A healthy Amazon account should generate 60 to 70 percent of its sales from organic searches and 30 to 40 percent from ad searches once the majority of its ad campaigns have been optimized. Ads alone cannot create this happy ratio, because Sellers must continually listen to their customers and improve on their products *every time* they buy more from their suppliers. Order metrics and customer service metrics must also be maintained. However, with the right product and a healthy margin, this split of Organic Sales to Ad Sales is sustainable *and* profitable. If done right, it will provide consistent sales growth and a TACoS that is small enough to maintain the overall growth and profitability of your business.

CHAPTER SUMMARY

- In less than a decade, Amazon ads have become an integral part of a Seller's success on the platform, with choice digital real estate given primarily to ad-sponsored products.

- In 2013, the cost-per-click (CPC) rate was as low as a nickel a click. By 2020, high-volume keywords were as high as $17 per click.

- Amazon Ads are important because when a paid keyword converts to a sale for your listing, the search algorithm adds relevance and links that keyword to your product. If you get enough sales driven by that keyword, then Amazon's search ranking algorithm will not only give your ads better placement for less money, it will also help your product rank in the organic search results.

- As of the writing of this book, there are four types of pay-per-click Amazon Ads available to Third-Party Sellers: (1) Sponsored Brands, (2) Sponsored Ads, (3) Sponsored Display, and (4) Amazon DSP

- The key to success lies in measuring your results. Tracking them on a daily basis can mean the difference between Amazon success and bankruptcy.

- "Cast a Wide Net" is an important strategy in ad success on Amazon because it trains the Amazon search algorithm to recognize your product and give over the prime digital real estate it deserves on the platform.

- Build up your ad budget war chest prior to launch. Your Amazon listings are an investment and you can't add them to your balance sheet until they gain relevance and rank.

Chapter 10:

BUILDING YOUR BRAND *OFF* AMAZON

"SELL TO BUILD YOUR BRAND,
DON'T BRAND TO CREATE SALES."

DAN KENNEDY

U p to this point in the book, the marketing methods and strategies shared have been concentrated on finding a winning product, researching the competition in a suitable category, then positioning a product to get ahead in the rankings on Amazon by creating a great listing, and finally driving traffic to it. When I first met Rick, I was more than a decade into my Amazon experience, and I had established myself as a Top 200 Seller because of my knowledge of how to navigate the Amazon.com platform. My product research techniques could be relied upon to consistently identify products with selling potential, and I was especially good at capitalizing on that potential because I paid close attention to the customer reviews and used that feedback to make key improvements that helped me leap-frog my products ahead of others in the same categories. My brothers would tell you that I was successful on Amazon because of my obsession *with* Amazon. But what I hadn't fully considered, until I met Rick, was that I could be even better on Amazon if I got better *off* of it. Rick taught me to think more like an entrepreneur by expanding my game plan outside the Amazon ecosystem, where there are even more opportunities to tell my story and cultivate my own database of happy customers eager to learn about my next product.

The transition to developing a more robust off-Amazon marketing strategy was a lot easier than I imagined, and the impact of this more holistic approach was nearly instantaneous. Over the next few pages, Rick will talk about some of his favorite off-Amazon channels and how to leverage these other platforms to boost your performance on Amazon, starting with a quick overview of direct response marketing. Here's Rick.

WHAT IS DIRECT RESPONSE MARKETING?

Before Jason ever dreamed of selling sports equipment online, I was selling products using direct response tactics I picked up selling sun screen to Florida sun lovers in the 1980s. While I wasn't the first by a long stretch to use direct response strategies (think Sears, Roebuck and Co. direct mail catalog, circa 1893), I was the first to use the concept successfully in long-form TV advertising called infomercials in the early 1990s. The concept is simple: direct response marketing uses a Call to Action (CTA) to trigger an immediate response from a targeted audience. That action may be to buy your product from Amazon; or maybe it's designed to get prospective customers to visit your website for more information. The title of my first book, *Buy Now!* pretty much sums it up, but I especially love Dan Kennedy's quote at the top of this chapter. Dan was one of my most influential mentors and a true pioneer in the direct marketing business, authoring a series of books called the *No B.S. Guides*. The quote,

"Sell to build your brand, don't brand to create sales," is from his book, *The No B.S. Guide to Brand Building by Direct Response*, and it truly captures the essence of DR marketing.

But selling is just part of the direct response equation. If you spend money on advertising, you need to be able to measure the amount of sales generated from that ad spend because *all direct response marketing is measurable*. This is sometimes called *accountable advertising*, which is tied to the concept of Return on Investment or ROI. Over many years in the business, I've developed a general rule for what your ROI should be, if you're going to be in a position to build brand awareness. Regardless of the type of marketing you use, aim for a 2 to 1 ROI. For every $1 spent on advertising, expect $2 back. This simple advertising concept works across every platform, and it can be your most powerful tool for getting ahead. Many of the products I've worked with over the years had very modest ad budgets, if any. We made certain that the money spent made money back, a direct response mindset that powers all of my campaigns.

I've always loved working with businesses that are already selling their products through multiple channels, not just Amazon alone. This usually means the business is spending advertising dollars outside Amazon. *Any money spent off Amazon for advertising will always help your Amazon sales.* This is a crucial point to recognize and understand because always holds true. While, as Jason learned early on, Amazon is the very best place to start selling your products, I'll show you how to boost your sales momentum off Amazon.

Sell to Brand: The Powerizer Story
When a large Fortune 500 consumer packaged goods (CPG) company launches a new product, they'll typically spend millions on a brand awareness campaign, hoping people will try their new product and create a buzz. But most inventors, entrepreneurs, and small businesses I know

do not have marketing budgets like that. A good example of a small company using brand awareness ads and struggling to grow early on is a product called Powerizer. The company was founded by a good friend of mine, Max Appel, founder of OxiClean. Years ago, I helped Max with the initial marketing for Oxiclean and some of their other products. Max's latest product, Powerizer, is an all-purpose cleaner designed to replace *all* of the other cleaners in your home.

Until recently, Max was using an agency that did not understand direct response marketing. Money was being spent across multiple channels, but the total sales volume wasn't growing. The agency was also managing Amazon, generating around $7,000 a month in sales. Max called me to ask for help. By now you can probably guess my first move: I called Jason to review the product's Amazon presence! He said they were doing a good job, with little room for improvement, so I took a close look at their website and at the advertising they were doing, and I recommended three simple changes.

Create your Unique Selling Proposition. The ads that were running for Powerizer were not delivering a clear, consistent message. They focused on how the product could replace all of the cleaners in your home and save you money. But that was hard for people to believe because there are so many specialty cleaners on the market. Powerizer was trying to be everything to everybody, but that's not how marketing works. I went back to the beginning, drafting a very short list of this product's best attributes. First, it truly is an all-in-one cleaner, something shoppers needed to better visualize. Secondly, it contains all natural ingredients, something more consumers want in their cleaning products. We created a new USP underscoring these two key points. It reads like this: "Powerizer cleans the toughest stains, but it's safe for you and your family." Our new ads showed five different cleaning demonstrations for the most common household spills and stains—and people started to respond.

Direct Response. Next, I changed the nature of the ads from a brand awareness campaign to direct response or conversion ads. In the earlier ads, there was no call-to-action. Our ads showed the product at work and we offered a 10% discount if you "order now!" This also drove up the response.

Target marketing. Finally, I focused all the brand awareness ad dollars being spent on multiple direct response ads on Facebook and Instagram. Once these platforms produce a positive ROI, then we can expand to others. The primary goal is to get Powerizer into people's hands because once they've tried it they'll be hooked!

Over the next few months, sales from the website began to increase on a daily basis until we were soon making money. Our targeted advertising "wins" allowed us to spend more each month. As these sales were growing, with very small changes to the Amazon listings, Amazon sales started increasing as well. Over the course of the next six months, Amazon sales grew from the original $7,000 a month to more than $40,000 a month as a direct result of the off-Amazon advertising we had employed. It bears repeating: *any money spent off Amazon for advertising will always help your sales on Amazon.*

OMNICHANNEL MARKETING

Until Amazon came along, there was only "off-Amazon marketing," so for me the argument for adding off-Amazon marketing seems flip-flopped. The way I see it, Amazon is just one more channel in the omnichannel universe. Today's consumer has seemingly unlimited options for how and where to purchase products and services. In response, I believe Sellers should expand their reach to *meet people where they are* in a way that provides consumers with a seamless and integrated shopping experience from the first touchpoint to the last. To cast a wider net, you've got to use a multichannel, or omnichannel approach to marketing your products, with Amazon as just one of the many possibilities.

I like to use the analogy of an iceberg when I talk with new clients about selling on Amazon. Think of Amazon as the tip of the iceberg, its most visible part. For that reason alone it should not be ignored. But to think of what's most visible as the most important part of your marketing strategy would be a big mistake, just like the dangers that can arise at sea from ignoring the even larger mass of ice below the surface. That mass is the foundation of the iceberg, just like the broader scope of your marketing plan provides the stability necessary for launching a successful marketing campaign. Losing sight of that can be a fatal error.

At the center of this diagram is your e-commerce website, from which traffic is pushed to and from numerous other channels. Amazon is regularly at the bottom-end of the funnel, where most shoppers go to purchase products. Where Amazon is not as strong, however, is in the area of discovery, where customers tend to rely instead on social media and other advertising channels to learn about a product or service, especially in the areas of clothing and beauty. This gets me back to my earlier point about meeting customers where they are. I call this being "sales agnostic," something both Jason and I consider ourselves to be first and foremost. If shoppers are learning about brands like yours in other-than-Amazon channels, then *that's where you need to be.* It really doesn't matter at the end of the day whether your product is purchased on Amazon or directly through your website. The more discovery you can stir up around your brand, the better.

Another big benefit that comes from utilizing multiple marketing channels is *synergy*—when the forces of using multiple channels begin to play off each other and, suddenly, 2+2 is greater than 4. I first experienced this synergistic effect when I was running Trillium Health Products, maker of the Juiceman juicer. We had a robust public relations strategy, infomercials, live seminars, and a book about to come out. This multi-channel "buzz" created a word-of-mouth side effect that exceeded the marketing we were actually doing. This impact was reflected in exponential year over year growth in sales. I got to experience this same exciting phenomenon with marketing campaigns for Sonicare, OxiClean, and GoPro years after selling Trillium.

Assuming you've followed the steps in the previous chapters of this book, and you're now feeling confident about the selling potential of your product, it's not uncommon to feel uneasy about where to start your marketing campaign, especially in today's marketplace hotbed. Considering the importance of getting off to a good start, both in terms of available resources and the pressure to create sales, I thought I'd take you through the same steps that Jason and I take our clients through, when we are helping them form their sales and brand-building strategies.

CONTROL THE NARRATIVE

Building a great website is critically important, and it's where I like to start with all of my clients. Amazon simply doesn't offer enough real estate to effectively build the content required for expanding your business. You can invest a lot of time into creating A+ listings, with all the bells and whistles, but without a link to "home base," where you've got the elbow room to tell the whole story, you're business will likely fall short of the big homerun.

Earlier in the book, we talked about the importance of controlling the conversation about your brand. Jason mentioned one of the fundamental mistakes people make: They take their products off Amazon—even big brands like Birkenstock—usually because they become frustrated with the platform's price-slashing tactics. The big problem with pulling out, as Jason explained earlier, is that you're not there to control the narrative about your products. I think the Birkenstock story is a great example because, when they pulled their products from the Amazon platform, they interrupted the flywheel effect and surrendered control of their messaging on the biggest e-commerce stage in the world. As a direct result, the knockoffs now own the Birkenstock void on Amazon, and that degrades the Birkenstock brand.

In Chapter 7, I mentioned the sisters who created Puriya and the turn-around they experienced when they re-tooled their website to focus on the benefits of their wonderful products, with gorgeous photography to underscore their messaging. The Puriya website gave them room to spell out their authentic story, from where they are now building strong ties to their customer base, seeding that word-of-mouth bonus effect I referenced earlier.

Key essentials for your online store
- ✓ Sign up with Shopify and set up your online shop
- ✓ Choose a theme or layout, then add your products to the store
- ✓ Tell your back story
- ✓ Establish your Unique Selling Proposition (USP)
- ✓ Include authentic product testimonials

Another plug for video

I was a biology major in college, and I've always had a special interest in how the human brain works. I am fascinated by the ways in which we are open to suggestion as a factor of our psychological makeup. I learned somewhere along the way that the brain has the ability to process visual content 60,000 times faster than it can process written text. That stuck with me, and it influenced my early use of television and video as effective marketing tools. Today using video is easier than ever, with tools at our fingertips for making them quickly and inexpensively. In this video-first society, there's really no excuse not to be putting video to work for you all of time. Here are the videos I recommend everyone have on their e-commerce website:

- If you are selling a product, the very first video on your website should be a short "sizzle video" for that product or for your brand (1-2 minutes). The video should quickly inform people about your product (or brand), what problem it solves, and why it is different from the competition. Think of it as a video commercial. Statistics show that people prefer to get this information in video rather than read it in text format.

- Always include a video about your origin story. Tell your customers why you got started in business and what inspired you to build your own brand. People like to know why you do what you do, and this 1-minute background story is shown to move people to purchase. Make it available on your "About Us" page.

- Always include testimonial videos on your website. I believe an authentic testimonial video can be one of your most powerful marketing tools because they are the best way to overcome objections and establish credibility and social proof.

- Seeing is believing and nothing sells a product better than a good demonstration video. Explain to people what problem your product solves, then spell it out in a short video. When

Jason swapped out his features-focused photos for aspirational images of real people interacting with his game tables, his sales skyrocketed. The effect was magnified when he applied the same technique to his videos.

5 Steps to Creating An Effective Demonstration Video
1. Introduce your product or your brand
2. Tell us who your product is for
3. Demonstrate how the product is used (show close-ups)
4. Cover the main features of the product, backed by benefits to the end-user
5. Use a specific Call-to-Action for purchase of your product from your website or from Amazon

I guarantee that if you include the videos described above, both your sales and conversions will go up, and you will begin to foster the kind of brand awareness and customer loyalty that can take your sales even higher. Plus, all of the video content on your e-commerce site can be repurposed for use on your Amazon listings and Amazon Brand Page. For more in depth information about using video on your website (and on Amazon), please check out *Video Persuasion,* my third book on how to create effective high-level product and testimonial videos that grow your brand, listed on the Resources page in the back of this book.

BUILD YOUR DATABASE

Think about your website and database as two legs of a three-legged stool, with Amazon as the third leg. This trio forms a solid marketing base from which you can effectively drive traffic to and from Amazon and your website. One of the benefits of selling through your own site is that *you now own customer information.* Growing your database through your own Shopify site, for example, with a good email-marketing system, will add value to your overall brand, guaranteed. In my experience, email is perhaps your most important asset. If you have a good, active, growing email list, you can control the information from your customer base and use it to drive traffic to Amazon listings or to your own website. This is especially important because no matter how successful you are on Amazon, you'll never know who is buying your products. That's not information Amazon is ever going to divulge. And without the ability to build a relationship with the people who are buying your products, you can't engage them proactively when your next product is in the queue.

Natural Stacks: A case study in database marketing
Several years ago I was asked to join the board of advisors for a new Seattle-based startup called Natural Stacks, a brain-health supplement company. Founders Roy Krebs and Ben Hebert launched the brand by first appearing on several popular podcasts, including The Tim Ferriss Show, ranked #1 for business podcasts. This initial exposure gave people the opportunity to try the Natural Stacks products *risk-free* through a special offer. From the very start, they focused on building their database of inquiries into loyal customers, beginning with their main product, Ciltep (now called Neuro Fuel). Once someone became a customer, they would email new content nearly every day. Then, every 5-7 days, a new product promotion was emailed. Using this approach, the company grew its list of loyal followers and leveraged the data to grow their brand. As a result, they've enjoyed year over year growth and have been able to expand to retail chains nationwide. If you want to see email marketing done right, go to their website and sign up to receive their product offers.

CONTENT MARKETING

Content marketing generally does not involve direct sales. Rather, it involves the creation of online material (such as videos, blogs, and social media posts) designed to stimulate interest and build rapport with your audiences. While it can be time-consuming to create, it can also be repurposed. A section of your blog post, for example, can be used on Facebook and/or added to your website. I've recently started converting blogs into online courses on topics you've been reading about here! If you're a one-person business, you've got to pace yourself, but I guarantee your efforts will be rewarded with new business if you can spread your message further.

Write a Book! Writing a book is the ultimate in content marketing. Doing so can establish your credibility as an expert in your field, while also leading to surprising opportunities that can take you in new and exciting directions. I have concentrated my marketing efforts around building authentic brands through multiple channels—all of them focused on telling a story and fostering trust. But most marketing channels are limited in the amount of content you can include when developing your story. The aim instead is to grab the customer's attention quickly, in as few choice words as possible, with a focus on the product benefits and a persuasive call to action. A book obviously gives you more room to expand. There are three ways to get published and in writing my first three books I've explored all of them: (1) traditional publishing, (2) hybrid publishing, and (3) self-publishing. They each have their pros and cons, depending on your resources and objectives for writing the book in the first place. The biggest marketing advantage of having a book, in my opinion, is additional traction you get through third-party press appearances, which provide yet another channel for telling your story and building your brand.

Public Relations: I've always been a big advocate of using PR to grow sales. Whether you do it yourself or hire a firm, there's frankly no better way I know of for driving good, credible traffic to your website (or to Amazon) because people tend to believe a story from a credible third-party source. Strategic media publicity placement is about getting your brand on mainstream TV shows and into magazines and newspapers your target audience knows and trusts. This media exposure amps up all of your Amazon activities because people are seeing and hearing about your brand more often, and this "positive familiarity" perpetuates trust. Additionally, media publicity creates news that journalists want to report. Don't fall for the trap that you only have news when you introduce a new product. Medical research, retail trends, fashion, celebrity activities, and seasonal interests all make good news. If you help journalists see and develop stories, they will report them, magnifying your message to prospective customers. These outside "endorsements" add to the believability of your brand and reinforce your customers' decision to purchase your product. A great marketing campaign, when amped by publicity, generates millions more impressions of all types.

Podcasts: Relevant podcasts are one of my favorite ways to drive traffic. They don't cost anything, and a podcast interview is an ideal format for introducing new people to your company. It's a great way to build your email list, too, and drive traffic to your website and to Amazon. The long-form format of most podcasts (30-45 minutes) provides a unique "space" for talking about your products, your business, and your story, with a podcaster people trust. Podcasters always give you an opportunity to direct people to take a specific action, too, whether asking listeners to call a certain number, send an emailing to receive a special offer, or directing them to Amazon to make a purchase. The field is pretty unlimited in terms of the topics being picked up by podcasters, including business, entertainment, music, health, politics, and education, to name just a few. You can book them yourself or there are services that book them for you. Check out our Resources page at the back of the book for contact information that can help you get started.

Influencers: Influencer marketing is another growing category in social media involving endorsements and product placements from "people of influence," usually people who have an expert-level of knowledge in their field and a large following on social media. Influencers are a great, usually inexpensive, way to drive traffic back to your website (or to Amazon). Many influencers have a website that they've turned into an affiliate page for Amazon, so when they drive traffic and sales from their website (or social media channels) to your Amazon listing, and it turns into a sale, not only does their influence grow in category, but they get paid by Amazon. The bigger the influencer follower list, the more expensive they may be to use. I recommend offering your product in exchange for their influence. The testimonials that come from these kinds of exchanges are priceless.

In Chapter 7, I talked about Jason's role in giving Vesta Precision a huge sales bump on Amazon by re-working their product listings. I was involved with Vesta from a different angle. In Miami there's a popular influencer named Guga, who has a YouTube channel with more than 700,000 followers. He calls it *Sous Vide Everything!* My team recently reached out to Guga to make some videos for the Vesta Precision products. Every time Guga does a video and releases it to his subscribers, sales of Vesta products—*on and off Amazon*—skyrocket. It may be worth noting that Amazon is now building its own influencer network on the Amazon platform. It's still in the early stages, but they're trying to get brands to communicate and work closely with influencers there. They obviously see the potential in driving sales through Influencers.

Google Ads: While 46% of most shopping-related searches begin on Amazon, the 35% that originate on Google should not to be ignored. Conversion rates or queries originating on Google will not be as high as those on Amazon, but this channel offers Sellers top-of-funnel discoverability that is too good to ignore. Google ads are excellent at matching keywords, images, and video, and they offer a wide-range of placements on their own properties, as well as on ad exchange networks. While Google's Search Network can reach people who are actively searching products, their Display Network can help you capture attention even *before* they start searching for what you have to offer. Combine that with powerful audience targeting and remarketing and you have a winning formula.

Facebook & Instagram Ads: Facebook is all about communities and connections, so it's not surprising then that their ads are geared toward targeting audience profiles, behaviors, and interests more than keywords. Since Facebook literally knows us through what we like, dislike, or ignore, it is perfectly suited for creating look-alike audiences that meet the specifications of our ideal avatars. A giant in its own right, Instagram is a great way to advertise products right in the feed. With the powerful data backing of its parent company, Facebook, reaching interest-based audiences is easier than ever. Creative marketers can also reach shoppers through influencer promotions, joint promotions, and takeovers.

TikTok: With 800 million users and growing, "addictive" is probably the best way to describe this short-form video app. While questions around safety of use from a data security perspective remain unanswered, Tik Tok continues to suck crowds in and keep them happy and engaged. This makes it a perfect environment for monetization, except that TikTok isn't ready for that yet. Many brands are slowly beginning to jump on the bandwagon, ready for when advertising is available on this millennial-focused platform. After all, brands must follow their audiences wherever they go!

CLEAN KEY: A CASE STUDY

A great example of a simple product that has used off-Amazon ads to build its business and its Amazon presence is another client of ours called Clean Key. Clean Key is a small device that allows you to open doors, push buttons, or punch a key-pad without touching any of those surfaces with your hand or finger. It came to prominence during the COVID-19 pandemic, but they didn't launch on Amazon. Clean Key experienced massive success with Facebook ads driving sales to a landing page. They hired me to help with a series of direct response television ads, and the success of these ads helped them get into both online and brick and mortar retail stores, like Walgreens, 7-Eleven, and GNC. They've done very well on Amazon too, mainly because of their off-Amazon ad spend. The key (no pun intended) to their success is being able to create ads that paid for themselves, then expand the business through multiple channels, just like we've been talking about in this chapter.

CHAPTER SUMMARY

- Customers like choices and while a majority of shoppers prefer Amazon, the Amazon.com platform limits the amount of content you can share about your product or service.

- Used in isolation, Amazon alone is not the best place to build your brand. Off-Amazon marketing gives you the real estate necessary to tell your story and leverage that information across multiple marketing channels so you can always be where your customers are.

- The omnichannel marketing model also has the advantage of economies of scale, where the same core set of information can be easily repurposed for use on other channels, giving the brand greater visibility for a broader customer base.

- *All direct response marketing is measurable.* As a rule of thumb, $1 in ad-spends should generate $2 in sales.

- Advertising dollars spent off-Amazon *will always increase your Amazon sales.*

- As you think about expanding your marketing reach off Amazon, be sure to start with the two fundamental platforms: your e-commerce site and your database. These core channels are essential for building a winning brand and they will fuel your Amazon business, not detract from it.

CONCLUSION

"NOTHING IN THE WORLD IS WORTH HAVING
OR WORTH DOING UNLESS IT MEANS EFFORT,
PAIN, DIFFICULTY...I HAVE NEVER IN MY LIFE ENVIED
A HUMAN BEING WHO LED AN EASY LIFE."

TEDDY ROOSEVELT

FIRE. READY. AIM.

Amazon was built off the backs of millions of hard working, creative Third-Party Sellers. If Amazon hopes to continue its rapid growth into the future, it will continue to be dependent on these very same people. Jeff Bezos and his team of executives deserve a lot of credit for guiding Amazon to where it is today. He and the company will also benefit greatly by giving more credit where credit is due—to 3P Sellers. Too many Sellers are denied due process before their listings, their accounts, and their livelihoods are struck down by Amazon. Sure, there is a small percentage of Sellers who are bad actors and for whom systems should be in place to weed them out. But there are far more genuine Sellers on the platform, operating within the Amazon Terms of Service, while also outperforming Amazon in retail sales. Ironically, Amazon's broken response to punishing *the bad guys* often hurts honest Sellers first. I often ask myself if Amazon has lost its way, with its authoritarian-style systems, or if it has just evolved into the kind of bureaucratic jungle for which it is named. The answer is probably a little of both.

When a client with a well-known kitchenware brand and several big-name customers tried to register for an Amazon Seller account recently, they were denied. Five months later, after repeated submissions of account documents, Amazon admitted they could not view the totality of the required documents that had been uploaded into their own Seller Central system. After we resubmitted the documents yet again, an Amazon representative told us that the reason the account had been in limbo was because the photocopies were not in color. Wait. What? I'd lived some of these crazy "Catch 22" explanations in the Marines, especially in regard to paperwork. But Amazon was supposed to be different.

THE DREADED *FALSE POSITIVE*

Nothing vexes good Amazon Sellers like the dreaded "false positive." When a handful of bad actors increased prices for essential items during the COVID-19 crisis, Amazon began an ill-conceived AI sweep of tens of thousands of listings targeted for price gouging. One of my clients, Vesta Precision, got rolled up in this mess and was wrongly deactivated—without notice. To add insult to injury, Vesta had actually been *reducing* their prices over the previous six months. It took six weeks before we were able to get all 12 of their top-selling items re-listed and re-ranked. In the meantime, the company's premium sous vide cookers and vacuum-sealing products, which had been selling at a record pace before the pandemic, lost sales and rankings, pushing them to the brink of ruin.

Luckily, together with specialist and friend Chris McCabe, we were able to get the company's listings reinstated and re-ranked quickly and in good standing. Many small business Sellers, however, don't have the necessary resources to fix these kinds of problems—problems that shouldn't exist in the first place.

I've been involved with Amazon for nearly 20 years, and these kinds of complications still vex me. Imagine how new Sellers must feel, with the least amount of experience and fewest financial resources to bounce back. I've been increasingly outspoken about these issues over the past few years, using my position of authority on the topic to draw more attention to these injustices and demanding change. I've also developed a reputation with Amazon beat reporters as a plain speaker, who isn't afraid to speak up for Sellers. Most Sellers are terrified of pushing back against Amazon for fear of retribution. I was still a Seller when I started raising a fuss, and I remember that fear vividly. Ironically, taking Amazon to task in the press seems to be the only way to get them to take corrective action. It certainly isn't going to happen with a support ticket.

READY. AIM. FIRE.

Only Amazon holds all of the cards on their e-commerce platform. The Seller is never in control. Our goal in creating *The Amazon Jungle Seller's Survival Guide* is to help you succeed on Amazon by being organized in your approach and disciplined in the execution of your long-term survival plan. Creating, nurturing, and growing your own private-label brand on Amazon is the safest, most reliable strategy there is for charting a path through a fearsome terrain. It won't prevent Amazon Basics from copying your product and undercutting you on price, but if you follow the tactics presented in this *Survival Guide* for making a great product and merchandising your listings, *you can beat Amazon at its own game*. Just ask our friend Bernie Thompson of Plugable, who continues to beat the pants off Amazon with his computer docking stations. Bernie is exactly the kind of rule-abiding, professional Seller to whom Amazon should be reaching out to before making hasty decisions that harm its Seller Community.

As I write this final chapter, the entire human race is in the throes of a global pandemic and Amazon is prospering. As brick and mortar businesses and retail stores are shuttered, Amazon and Amazon Sellers are providing much needed goods to help people endure this crisis. Even as the e-commerce giant stumbles with longer delivery times and inventory shortages, Amazon.com is poised to exit this crisis stronger and more powerful than it was pre-pandemic because there is no other online retail platform that comes close to their resources and services. But there are dark clouds on the horizon.

Over the past few years, antitrust lawyers and policymakers have been circling the giant, and for good reason given their growing market share. As consumers in a free country, we have to ask ourselves whether one company with the power of Amazon is good for American consumers and small businesses? While I'm no legal scholar, I do have a couple of recommendations for our policymakers that I've spelled out below.

Report total dollar value of goods sold

In Chapter 1 I talk about how Amazon skirts the truth in its sales reporting by only disclosing the fees it charges 3P Sellers, rather than the full retail value of goods sold on their platform, known as Gross Merchandise Value (GMV). Considering that more than half of all Amazon sales are third-party sales, the sum value of what's *not* being reported is colossal and, when factored into the full equation, would reveal the true size and power of Amazon. It's high time that Amazon, and all public marketplace companies, share the true GMV with the public and its investors. Without this information, and without a legal requirement for Amazon to comply, how can we even begin to answer the question of monopoly? Our policy makers should require Amazon to share their sales numbers so that we can make apples-to-apples comparisons regarding just what kind of power they hold in each of their product and service categories. For example, what is Amazon's market share in the Toys category or Sporting Goods? What is Amazon's market share of total retail when you subtract out things Amazon doesn't sell, like automobiles. Let us see for ourselves whether the 4% of U.S. sales figure that Amazon management regularly throws out in the press is true and accurate. I certainly am not fooled.

What about safety?

Jeff Bezos built Amazon on the principle of customers first. Low prices and supreme convenience are two obvious ways Amazon lives up to its customer obsession. But what about safety? As a result of the 1996 Communication Decency Act (CDA), Section 230, Amazon, like Facebook, cannot be held liable for untrue, misleading, or unsafe products sold by users of its platform. Just as Facebook blatantly shirks responsibility for misleading and fact-less political ads on its platform, Amazon claims no responsibility for counterfeiters selling unsafe and harmful products on theirs. If Congress would act immediately to amend or eliminate Section 230 of the CDA, allowing injured shoppers to sue Amazon and win, I'm absolutely certain Amazon would find a solution to this problem with the speed and accuracy of Prime Now.

Most Sellers I know believe Amazon has too much power. Although Amazon management has publicly stated that Sellers can go elsewhere to make a living, I can tell you that they can't, if they want to grow a successful online business. When I sold the exact same product on other online marketplaces, the sum total of my sales on all of those platforms combined was less than 10% of our Amazon sales. These included reputable retailers, like Walmart.com, Sears.com, Jet.com, Rakuten, eBay, Newegg, and Houzz to name a few. All of them together still only amounted to a small fraction of our Amazon sales. Nearly every Seller I talk to has the same story. With Amazon, we're dealing with something truly unprecedented and it's nearly impossible to survive without them.

Earlier in the book I shared part of this quote from Charles Munger, an American investor, business man, former real estate attorney, and philanthropist. He is also vice chairman of Berkshire Hathaway, the conglomerate controlled by Warren Buffett. Mr. Munger himself said that *there has hardly ever been anything like it [Amazon] in the history of our country.* He went on to say that *he would not have predicted the success that has happened,* and now that it has happened, he said *he wouldn't want to predict that it was going to stop either.*[19] With power comes great responsibility, but also the potential for corruption, even by the most well-meaning individuals or groups. I would like to think that if Amazon took a hard, unbiased look at just how much Third-Party Sellers have helped them get to where they are today, they would #DoBetterAmazon. Sellers deserve it.

SEMPER GUMBY

I wrote this book for two reasons. I wanted to share my truth about Amazon and its ways because for 17 years I was a Third-Party Seller with indelible bruises to show for it. I know the kind of hardships Sellers face, and I know what it feels like to skip a paycheck (or more) in order to make payroll for your team, after your listing was unfairly pulled by Amazon. I've been there, and I learned the hard way. In the Marines we had to be flexible—always. "Semper Gumby" is a play on Semper Fidelis, which means "Always Faithful." When Captain Jay Farmer of HMM-264 actually flew with a Gumby character toy mounted on the instrument panel of his CH-46E, the term, first used in the mid-seventies, was popularized and a reminder to *literally* be flexible to survive. Success on

---

19 Catherine Clifford. "Warren Buffett's right-hand man Charlie Munger: Amazon is 'an utter phenomenon of nature.'" Make it. February 15, 2019. https:// www.cnbc.com/2019/02/15/berkshire-hathaways-charlie-munger-amazon-is-phenomenon-of-nature.html

Amazon, however, requires more than good faith and flexibility, which brings me to the second reason I wrote this book.

I want to help you build a winning brand. Rick Cesari and I both know what it's like to create a product and a company from nothing; products that provide value, meaning, and style in the marketplace. We've both experienced the deep satisfaction of connecting with customers whose lives are better because they bought our products. By listening to their demands and following their recommendations, we are making a positive difference on and off the Amazon.com platform. By following the strategies in our *Seller's Survival Guide*, you can too.

Amazon may be big and scary at times, but with the right strategy it's still the best place to launch, list, and learn about your product in order to perfect it. Once you make those critical product improvements, expanding to other online sales channels and retail stores is much, much easier. Before I'd fully exited my Amazon business and transitioned to Avenue7Media, I kept getting calls from major retailers like Home Goods and Wayfair, even though I was no longer actively looking to sell to them. They found my brand on Amazon because my brothers and I had done things the right way, with the right strategies, and with great, quality products that customers raved about even after we were gone. With the right strategy, some grit and determination, you too can begin your business on Amazon and watch it grow far beyond the limits of the *everywhere store*.

Third-Party Sellers are the untold story of Amazon's success. By building an enduring brand—one that is recognized on and off the platform—your voice will be amplified and, eventually, Amazon will listen. Rick and I have created a list of resources on the next page to help you get started. With these tools, plus the sales and marketing strategies we've shared in this book, we believe you have what it takes to navigate the Amazon Jungle and clear your own unique path to prosperity. Now go build the next great twenty-first century brand!

BONUS PAGE/CALL TO ACTION

To engage with Jason regarding Amazon managed services or for consulting projects, please visit www.Avenue7Media.com.

To contact Jason about media appearances, podcasts, or speaking at your event you may reach him at info@avenue7media.com or via linkedin.com/in/jasonrboyce

To contact Rick about media appearances, podcasts, consulting projects or speaking at your event, or to subscribe to his Blog, visit: www.Rick-Cesari.com

CONNECT WITH RICK ON HIS SOCIAL MEDIA PLATFORMS:
Facebook: https://www.facebook.com/rickcesaridrtv/
Twitter: http://twitter.com/rickcesaridrtv
YouTube: https://rickcesari.tv
LinkedIn: https://www.linkedin.com/in/rickcesaridrtv/
Amazon: https://amazon.com/author/rickcesari

ABOUT THE AUTHORS

JASON BOYCE

Entrepreneur and nationally recognized expert on Amazon, Jason Boyce is considered one of the leading advocates for Amazon.com Third-Party Sellers. Jason began selling direct to consumers as an e-commerce retailer in 2002 and as a 3P Amazon Seller in 2003. He has bootstrapped several of his own brands to success with a 7-Step Method developed over a decade and a half of real-world trial and error. These methods helped Jason's company become a Top 200 Amazon Seller and a top 1,000 e-commerce seller according to Internet Retailer Magazine. In 2014, while speaking at several Amazon Selling and e-commerce conferences, Jason realized that helping others succeed was more meaningful than growing his own brands. He began supporting a small group of Sellers in 2015, which evolved into Avenue7Media, a 21st-century product marketing agency. Jason not only writes about business—he lives it! As an Amazon Top Seller for close to 20 years, he has accumulated extraordinary depth of experience and real-life understanding of the challenges Amazon 3P Sellers face. He has more recently become a go-to expert for media sources seeking to understand the Amazon experience from the Seller's point-of-view, including CNBC, PBS Frontline, *The Wall Street Journal*, Bloomberg News, *The New York Times* and *The Washington Post*.

RICK CESARI

When he was just 29 years old, Rick Cesari built Trillium Health Products, makers of the Juiceman Juicer and Breadman Bread Machine into a $75 million company in just four years. After selling Trillium, he devoted his knowledge and passion for marketing to help others build their businesses. He guided a company that made a slow-selling mini electric skillet called the Fajita Express to rebrand and sell it with a celebrity spokesman. Now known as the George Foreman Grill, it has sold more than 120 million units. GoPro began with a surfer selling the now-iconic camera out of the back of a Volkswagen bus. Rick used his direct response television marketing expertise, combined with online videos, to target consumers. The result? Another billion-dollar brand. With over 5 million sellers on Amazon, standing out from the pack is essential for long-term success. In this book, Rick walks you through his unique process of branding products through differentiation and messaging, providing a step-by-step *Seller's Survival Guide* for better reaching a society of consumers who connect to the virtual world of retail through Amazon. He is the author of three previous books, *Buy Now: Creative Marketing That Gets Customers to Respond to You and Your Product; Building Billion Dollar Brands: Spectacular Successes & Cautionary Tales;* and *Video Persuasion: Everything You Need to Know About How to Create Effective High-Level Videos.*

RESOURCES

WWW.AVENUE7MEDIA.COM/THEAMAZONJUNGLE
For quick access to sample plans and other instructions referenced in the book

Avenue7Media
www.avenue7media.com
Premier product launch & marketing agency. Jason Boyce, founder

Jason Boyce on LinkedIn.com/in/jasonrboyce and Twitter @JasBoyce

Rick Cesari
www.rickcesari.com
Premier DTC marketing consultant. Rick Cesari, founder.

Rick Cesari on LinkedIn/in/RickCesariDRTV and Twitter@rickcesaridrtv
Follow me on Facebook@rickcesaridrtv
Follow me on YouTube @rickcesari.tv

AMAZON ACCOUNT SET UP

IP Accelerator
https://brandservices.amazon.com/ipaccelerator
To help you find an IP Attorney to register your brand.

Seller Central Account Set Up
www.Avenue7Media.com/TheAmazonJungle

AMAZON PRODUCT & KEYWORD RESEARCH

AMZ Suggestion Expander
www.crx4chrome.com
A chrome extension to expand the number of search suggestions shown in the Amazon search bar.

Helium 10
www.helium10.com
A suite of insanely powerful SEO, product research, and business management tools for Amazon Sellers.

Jungle Scout Chrome Extension
www.junglescout.com
My favorite way to determine if a product is a worthwhile investment with accurate real-time data.

Keepa
www.keepa.com
This is an awesome tool that can help you make better buying decisions.

ManageByStats
www.managebystats.com
Makes management, reporting metrics, and tracking lot easier, more tangible and visible.

Infogroup
https://www.infogroup.com/
Identify you customer and know your data

Seller Labs
www.sellerlabs.com
Get access to the highest-ranking keywords for a product.

Sellics Reverse ASIN Tool
www.sellics.com/reverse/asin
Monitor your keyword rankings and see how your optimization efforts affect your rankings.

BOOKS

Cesari, Rick. *Video Persuasion: How to create high-level product and testimonial videos that will grow your brand, increase sales, and build your business.* (Publisher), 2019.

Cesari, Rick, and Barb Westfield. *Building Billion Dollar Brands: Spectacular successes & cautionary tales—the lure of brand response from both sides of the marketing fence.* Advantage, Charleston, South Carolina, 2018.

Cesari, Rick, and Ron Lynch, with Tom Kelly. *Buy Now: Creative marketing that gets customers to respond to you and your product.* John Wiley & Sons, Inc., Hoboken, New Jersey, 2011.

Cialdini, Robert B, PhD. *Influence: The psychology of persuasion.* Harper Collins, 1984.

Kennedy, Dan S, with Forrest Walden and Jim Cavale. *No B.S. Guide to brand-building by direct response: the ultimate no holds barred plan to creating and profiting from a powerful brand without buying it.* Enterprise Press, 2014.

Kim, Chan W, and Renee Mauborgne. *Blue Ocean Strategy: How to create uncontested market space and make the competition irrelevant.* Harvard Business School Publishing Corporation, 2015.

Sinek, Simon. *Start with Why. How Great Leaders Inspire Everyone to Take Action.* The Penguin Group, 2009.

Thomson, James, Ph.D. and Joseph Hansen. *The Marketplace Dilemma.* James Thomson, 2016.

Thomson, James, Ph.D. and Whitney Gibson. *Controlling your brand in the age of Amazon.* James Thomson, 2020.

FEATURED BUSINESSES & BRANDS

Andrew Waber
www.teikametrics.com

Chris McCabe
www.ecommercechris.com

James Thomson & Joseph Hansen
www.buyboxexperts.com

Jewelry Spa Hot Tub
www.jewelryspahottub.com

mumi
www.mumidesign.com

Natural Stacks
www.naturalstacks.com

Nutent Therapeutics
www.nutenttherapeutics.com

Plugable
www.plugable.com

Powerizer
www.powerizerclean.com

Puriya
www.puriya.com

Vesta Precision
www.vestaprecision.com

MANUFACTURING

Datamyne.com
A source for global import/export records.

ImportGenius.com
A source for global import/export records.

Panjiva.com
A source for global import/export records.

QIMA
Onsite supplier audit programs, product inspections, and laboratory tests for global bands, retailers, and importers.

Sample Inspection Check List
www.avenue7media.com/TheAmazonJungle

Sample Product Specifications Sheet (PSS)
www.avenue7media.com/TheAmazonJungle

Sample Request for Pricing (RFP)
www.avenue7media.com/TheAmazonJungle

Thomasnet.com
A leading product sourcing and supplier discovery platform.

MARKETING & ADVERTISING

PPC Ninja, Ritu Java
https://www.ppc.ninja/

Seller Labs
www.sellerlabs.com

Teikametrics
www.teikametrics.com

A data-driven platform that helps retailers optimize and win business online. Specializes in pricing optimization, operations, and inventory for Sellers of all sizes.

PODCASTS

10k Collective
Michael Veazey

Actualize Freedom
Danny Carlson

INspired INsider with Dr. Jeremy Weisz
Inspiredinsider.com

Interview Valet
The Category King in Podcast Interview Marketing

The Buy Box Experts Podcast
Joseph Hansen, James Thomson, Eric Stopper

The Jason & Scot Show Podcast
Jason "Retailgeek" Goldberg and Scot Wingo

CPSIA information can be obtained
at www.ICGtesting.com
Printed in the USA
JSHW042228041120
9328JS00007B/186